Very few coaches have been able to change cultures as quickly and successfully as Lon Kruger. He understands how to mold a group of individuals into one team with a common goal and has proven that time and time again. Lon has high standards for all those around him and he possesses a passion for winning, but not at any cost. That is arguably his strongest trait.

— LARRY BROWN
Charlotte Bobcats' Head Coach, winner of both NBA and NCAA championships
2004 U.S. Olympic Team Head Coach

Lon is a brilliant businessman, who just happens to coach basketball. While he is known for his humility, his desire to win and his competitive drive is second to none. That balance of sincere humility with unending competitiveness is a unique trait many of the world's premier business leaders share.

— STEVE AND ELAINE WYNN
Wynn Las Vegas

Lon Kruger understands business because he understands people. The business world missed out on an all-star when Lon went into coaching.

—BILL BOYD
Executive Chairman of the Board, Boyd Gaming Corporation

Lon Kruger helps to set the bar for integrity in our profession. His history of success in college basketball is even more impressive when you realize he has repeatedly revitalized programs all while operating strictly within the rules. Lon is a coach's coach. We all have something to learn from him.

— ROY WILLIAMS
Head Coach, University of North Carolina

Coach simply helps you be the best you can be — on and off the court. Players give their best because they know he cares.

— MITCH RICHMOND
Former All-American for Kruger at Kansas State and six-time NBA All-Star

Lon Kruger is one of the finest leaders of young men I have witnessed in nearly a quarter-century of covering college basketball for CBS. Moreover, he is a good man. It doesn't surprise me that he has been a proven winner time and time again. When you mix leadership with passion and integrity, you get Lon Kruger.

— JIM NANTZ
CBS Sports

A lot of guys are great coaches, but Coach Kruger is also a great person. He's our role model, the way he handles this team and his family and how he carries himself. He taught us basketball but also how to be a good human being. About life.

— CURTIS TERRY
Former UNLV point guard

As an elected official, I draw back on what I have learned from Lon Kruger. People don't want to hear about the negatives and what's going wrong. People want to know the truth, the facts, and what we can do to make things better. Throughout the years I have found myself thinking, 'What would Lon do in this situation?' I've also done this as a parent. I believe thinking this way has made me a better parent as well as a better elected official.

— CARL GERLACH
Mayor of Overland Park, Kansas and
a former Kansas State teammate of Lon Kruger

Coach Kruger's approach prepares his players for life beyond basketball. Over the years I have spoken about sports as representing a microcosm of life, including the business world, and present talks about the intertwining of both. As a result it is my strong conviction that a player coming out of Coach Kruger's program will have a solid foundation and be well positioned to become a major force in whatever endeavor he chooses.

— EDWARD KLEIN, MD
who has worked with teams in the NFL, NHL and Major League Baseball on
improving performance with the use of visualization

I had to trust Coach Kruger. He told me if I did redshirt (before my senior year), I would have a chance to continue my career after college, maybe even play in the NBA for many years. I think he had higher expectations for me than I did. He knew what I was capable of and wanted to make sure I could achieve as much as I could. As I look back, redshirting that season was the best thing that ever happened to me. Not only did we enjoy a special season when I finally did play my senior year at UNLV, it put me in a position to be where I am today . . . in the NBA.

— JOEL ANTHONY,
Miami Heat center and the 2007 Mountain West Conference
Defensive Player of the Year

TheXs&Osof
Success

Success is a Sport.

Peace –

Success is a Spirit.

– Peace –

The Xs & Os of Success

A Playbook for Leaders in Business and Life

Lon Kruger
and
D.J. Allen

Stephens Press ■ Las Vegas, Nevada

Editor: Steve Guiremand
Art Director: Sue Campbell
Cover photo: Louie Traub
Back cover photo: Jeff Scheid
Publishing Coordinator: Stacey Fott

Library of Congress Cataloging-in-Publication data

Kruger, Lon.
  The Xs & Os of success : a playbook for leaders in business and life /
Lon Kruger and D.J. Allen.
    272 p. ; 23 cm.

ISBN: 1-935043-03-X
ISBN-13: 978-1-935043-03-4

  The author presents forty lessons learned as a basketball coach which
apply to any leadership role and to life in general.
1. Leadership. 2. Basketball coaches. I. Title. II. Allen, D.J.

658.409/4 dc 22   2009   2008937490

STEPHENS PRESS, LLC
A Stephens Media Company

P.O. Box 1600 (89125-1600)
1111 West Bonanza Road
Las Vegas, Nevada 89106
(702) 386-5260
www.stephenspress.com

Printed in the United States of America

To the teammates who constantly make plays for us:
Barb, Angie and Kevin.
Stacey, Bailey and Daniel.
We love you.

Contents

Sincere Humility, Unending Competitiveness

Nothing brings the Las Vegas community together like UNLV Runnin' Rebel basketball. Our city is so unique, so vibrant, so diverse. People from all over the world come to this city to work, to play and to live. We all join together supporting one common interest when our Runnin' Rebels are winning at a high level.

For over 15 years, that feeling eluded this city. Then something magical happened in March of 2007. Lon Kruger's underdog Runnin' Rebel team captured the hearts and minds of those in this community as it shocked the college basketball world by advancing to the Sweet 16. UNLV basketball had climbed its way back onto the national stage — where it rightfully belongs.

However, that has not been Lon's biggest achievement in this city. What Lon has done to build the foundation for long-term success with his program is to engage an entire community. He understands his program is not, in fact, his. It belongs to the students, the professors, the boosters, the fans — it belongs to Las Vegas.

Lon is a master strategic partner. He has a vision of what his entity can do to help you and what your entity can do to help his. Win-win is not rhetoric — it is a way of life. Whether it is supporting education or healthcare, the local business economy or the homeless youth, Lon works tirelessly to support others.

But don't underestimate the value of the return on investment of these efforts. Lon is a brilliant businessman, who just happens to coach basketball. While he is known for his humility, his desire to win and his competitive drive are second to none. That balance of sincere humility with unending competitiveness is a unique trait many of the world's premier business leaders share.

Runnin' Rebel Fever is back in Las Vegas thanks to the CEO of UNLV basketball, Lon Kruger. Enjoy his lessons from this book. Remember, we are all coaches — and we must never stop coaching our teams.

— Steve and Elaine Wynn

Popcorn

Dad was my hero.

He taught me to love, he taught me to scrap and he taught me to respect. I am the man I am today — as a father, a husband and a coach — because of him.

The older I get the more I realize just how much he lived for his kids. Not through us, but for us. He wanted all of us kids to have more opportunities than he ever had — and his wish came true.

My childhood was near perfect. We grew up in the 800-person town of Silver Lake, Kansas, a short drive away from the capital city of Topeka.

Our lives evolved around one thing — sports. Baseball, in particular. Dad was a big baseball fan and I followed in his footsteps. Our summer vacations were spent barnstorming with our Little League teams as far north as Canada. What seemed like the entire town would pack up their cars and set out on a three-week journey to look for games in every town we came across. Looking back on it, there is not much more a young boy could ask for.

Sometimes Dad would coach as many as three baseball teams at a time — mine, and two of my younger brothers'. He would have to head from diamond to diamond to juggle his responsibilities and, somehow, he always made it happen without missing a beat.

My favorite memories of being with him are the days we would travel around to the different high schools in the area watching Silver Lake High's football, basketball and baseball teams. As the oldest, I was the first to go to these games with him.

I can still remember some of the names and the faces of Silver Lake's star players — as a ten-year-old boy those high schoolers were my idols. Gym after gym, field after field, game after game — it was so good to be around Dad.

Our routine during basketball season was the same. Arrive early, grab some popcorn and try to pick out the opposing team's starters just by watching them perform in their pre-game warm up. (Dad always won.) The smell of freshly prepared popcorn and the fun times with Dad was a tough combo to beat.

Our family also spent a lot of time together working the concession stand at the local ballpark — opening it up or staying until closing time and always talking sports with the familiar smell of fresh popcorn lingering in the air.

Dad is gone now, and I miss him dearly. But I try to carry with me to this day all of his teachings — many of which you will find in this book.

He was a strong man. So strong, in fact, that compassion was his greatest asset. He loved and respected others and tried to teach us kids to do the same. I hope we have delivered for him.

It's ironic to think I have made a career out of traveling to high school games and watching kids play hoping to find the right ones to come play in our programs. It seems like just yesterday I was watching those high school games with Dad.

Life has changed. Times have changed. Silver Lake is no longer our home, but a place we love to visit.

However, one thing hasn't changed — the smell of popcorn. To this day, it's the greatest smell in the world. Every time I smell popcorn, it reminds me of great times spent with the greatest man in my world, Dad.

I love you, Dad. Thank you for giving us your all.

— Lon Kruger

A Better Me

Lon Kruger stood amongst the members of the euphoric crowd, as if wanting to simply be a part of them rather than the subject of their adoration. But that would not be possible on this afternoon. Not while wearing his new crown, the one bestowed upon him as the new Mr. Las Vegas (with all due apologies to Wayne Newton and Mayor Oscar Goodman, of course).

Over the previous three months, his UNLV Runnin' Rebels had revived the alter ego of this city known around the world for skin and sin. Las Vegas had become a closet college basketball town. Why closet? Well, Las Vegas adores winners and that was something UNLV basketball had seemingly forgotten how to do on a national level.

Yes, college basketball had actually mattered in Las Vegas some fifteen years earlier. It mattered more than catchy marketing phrases or where Paris Hilton parties.

But a decade and a half is an eternity in the Implosion Capitol of the World. We count our years here like dogs count theirs. To us, the Bellagio is already a historic landmark. (No, not that Landmark. They imploded that Landmark.) And, in the blink of an eye, the much maligned departure of Jerry Tarkanian in 1992 led to a run of mediocre UNLV teams and took college basketball from our front pages to the back of our minds.

Until now, that is, when Kruger's crew reminded us there is one thing that will bring this hodgepodge of a community together — Runnin' Rebel basketball. For a city made up of transplants and about 17 of us natives, UNLV basketball is the one thing we can all rally behind together.

And Kruger was the man to do it in just his third year in the desert. Here — in the land where we idolize champions — if you lead our Runnin' Rebels to national acclaim, this city is yours. Just tell us what you want.

So there stood Las Vegas' newest favorite son. The most unlikely of heroes in these parts — the son of a postal worker from a Kansas town smaller than one of our mega-resorts' parking structures.

His squad had just completed a ferocious 13-point come-from-behind victory over rival BYU to capture the 2007 Mountain West Conference Tournament championship at the Thomas & Mack Center just minutes from The Strip. The win guaranteed the Runnin' Rebels — who were nationally ranked for the first time since 1992 — a berth in the NCAA Tournament. This fantastic voyage — with a sea of Rebel red following — would continue all the way to the Sweet 16.

But for now, that sea of red was converged on the floor of the T&M cheering the Rebels' players on as they took turns cutting off their respective pieces of the championship twine. In the middle of it all Kruger was taking congratulatory handshakes and hugs as if his name was on a ballot. See, that's what happens when your Runnin' Rebels win. Rock stars have nothing on you in the City of Lights.

I had slowly made my way to the bottom rows of the seats relishing every moment. The players celebrated with the student body on the court while the assistant coaches shared the accomplishment with their families.

Selfishly, I wanted my moment with Coach Kruger. We had built a professional working relationship over the past year, one based on public outreach and marketing opportunities for him and the team.

We had actually first met almost two years to the day earlier in a chance meeting at a local movie theater. I introduced myself that day as a life-long Runnin' Rebel fan and UNLV graduate and thanked him and his wife, Barb, for coming to Las Vegas. That was not a sentiment they were hearing much at the time as many fans had already written his program off after a lone season. But I felt I had seen a glimpse of the future during the final stretch of that 2004-05 season. It was something most people are too afraid to see — hope.

Now, two years later, my personal investment in hope was returning dividends. And today was payday.

However, I had to be honest with myself. No doubt this would probably be the beginning of a new era for King Kruger in Las Vegas. And peasants like me — a fan with big dreams but minimal resources — would soon be replaced with big names and faster times. But, I thought, it was fun while it lasted.

I made my way onto the court, working through the crowd before waiting for my turn to talk to the man everyone else in the building wanted to speak with. He met me with his familiar smile and — like I had told him two years earlier — I simply said, "Thank you for coming here, Coach."

His response was classic Kruger, putting me before him. "Did you enjoy that, D.J.?" he asked as we did that half-handshake, half-hug thing guys do after select accomplishments.

"It was great, Coach," I said. "Thank you. Thank you . . . for everything."

That was all I needed to say. That would be my happy ending to my Runnin' Rebel fantasy.

I had turned to head home — alone. To watch the replay of the game deep into the night, call my friends to discuss the win and have my wife get sick of me talking about the game and, for that matter, the entire season.

Or so I thought. That's when Coach called

out to me with six words that would forever change my life.

"D.J., we're going to Red Robin."

Seriously, Red Robin?

———

Known for its gourmet burgers, Red Robin is a place you expect to see champions dine — if those champions had just won some sort of Little League title and need to be in bed by eight because it's a school night. Most of us would assume NCAA coaching icons celebrate their big victories at places named after people like Fleming, Morton or Ruth's Chris.

Not Lon Kruger. He has a small dilemma with that scenario. The young children of his assistant coaches and others would not be able to order pizza and cheeseburgers at places like that.

But just because Kruger may not act like what most sports fans might envision a coaching legend should act like, does not mean he is not one of them.

In fact, when UNLV came within two baskets of advancing to the Elite Eight in the 2007 NCAA Tournament, Kruger cemented his place as the most successful change agent in college basketball history. Five times Kruger has taken over a program in need of rebuilding and five times his programs have reigned victorious within a span of just four years.

A 20-win season in his fourth and final year at Texas-Pan American. He also served as Pan American's athletic director — the youngest AD in the nation at the time (he was 29 when he was hired) — while also serving as a first-time head coach. The team had won only five games the year prior to Kruger taking over in 1982.

An Elite Eight appearance in his second season at Kansas State and four NCAA Tournament appearances in his four seasons coaching his alma mater. The Wildcats had not reached the tournament in the four seasons prior to Kruger taking over the program in 1986 and were just a combined one game over .500 in the three previous seasons. His 1987-88 team still holds a tie for the school's single-season record of 25 wins. The run under Kruger also marks the only time the Kansas State program went to the NCAA Tournament four consecutive seasons.

A Final Four appearance and a then-team record of 29 wins in his fourth season at Florida. The Gators were under investigation by the FBI and NCAA when Kruger took over the program in 1990, with the team coming off a seven-win season. The unofficial expectations were simple at the time — keep the Gators out of trouble and out of the headlines. In addition to cleaning up the program off the court, his teams went on

to win over 100 games in the next six years
with four postseason appearances, including a
magical run to the Final Four in 1994.

**A Big Ten title for Illinois in his second
season with the Fighting Illini and three
NCAA Tournament appearances in his
four seasons.** The Fighting Illini had not captured a Big Ten title in 12 years (and only one
in 33 years) when Kruger took over in 1996.
Illinois had also won just one NCAA Tournament game since 1989 and was under NCAA
sanctions when he arrived. Under Kruger,
the Illini advanced to the second round three
times in four seasons.

**A Sweet 16 appearance, a national
ranking, a Mountain West Conference
Tournament title and a 30-win season
in just his third season at UNLV in 2007.**
The once proud Runnin' Rebels had not won
a game in the NCAA Tournament since 1991
(with just two appearances in 15 years) and
had not been ranked nationally since 1992.
And despite losing four starters and five
seniors from the 2006–07 team, the 2007–08
squad — in a "rebuilding year" — went on to
win 27 games, repeated as conference tournament champions and returned to the second
round of the NCAA Tournament.

The names keeping company with Kruger
tell more of the story. Only four coaches ever
have led three different schools to the Sweet
16 since the NCAA Tournament expanded to

64 teams — Kruger, Rick Pitino, Bill Self and Tubby Smith.

Kruger is also just one of three coaches to lead four different schools to NCAA Tournament wins — Jim Harrick and Eddie Sutton are the others — and he is just one of five coaches to ever take four different schools to the NCAA Tournament — Lefty Driesell, Harrick, Pitino and Sutton join him. Kruger and Harrick are also the only two coaches in history to take four schools to the tournament at least twice each.

Detractors can say this track record showcases a lack of commitment to one school. But there is a valid reason for every time he left a program. There was the challenge of proving what he could do away from Kansas State, his alma mater, which was less than an hour from the small Kansas town of Silver Lake where he grew up. (This is something most professionals in their mid-30s can relate to.)

After a six-year run at Florida, a personnel issue with administration (you will find Kruger never publicly airs dirty laundry) forced him to move his program to Illinois in the Big Ten. And, of course, the lure of the challenge presented by the NBA led Kruger from the Fighting Illini to the Atlanta Hawks — a period of time when Kruger learned a lot about himself and the business of professional basketball.

And a sign of the greatest of leaders — he

always left the programs in better shape than when he found them. A foundation had been laid at Florida and Illinois for strong coaches — Billy Donovan and Self, respectively — to replace Kruger and enjoy amazing success with their teams. In fact, Self led Illinois to the Elite Eight in his first year with the Illini.

The fact is Kruger is and has been a wanted man in the basketball world. The rumors, and truths, of the college and professional teams that have come calling over the past 20 years to ask Kruger to help them rebuild are countless. (The names are big and the courting has been non-stop for two decades.) If Kruger didn't want to come back for his fourth or fifth seasons at UNLV, his bank account would have benefited and recruits would be more likely to answer the phone on a new school's name recognition alone. Forget interviews, the offers were there.

But Kruger is not the type of person who positions himself with the leverage of the people who want him. In fact, he believes this is disrespectful to the coaches who ultimately accept the jobs. He says they shouldn't be publicly known as the second or third choices. Thus, his name stays out of the headlines of the rumor mill as much as possible.

Because of his mentality of not seeking the spotlight, Kruger is not as celebrated as most sports figures of his generation. In fact, he is

more possibly known as his coaching generation's most-proven underdog.

In his signature seasons at Kansas State,
Florida, Illinois and UNLV (to this point),
each respective team entered the year with
minimal expectations before finishing the
season as a team that apparently "came out of
nowhere."

———

- His 1987-88 team at Kansas State
  advanced to the Elite Eight despite being
  picked to finish fourth in its own conference, the Big 8 (today's Big 12).

- The 1993-94 Florida Gators were picked
  eighth in the SEC but shocked the nation
  by advancing all the way to the Final
  Four.

- Kruger's 1997-98 Illinois squad was
  picked in the preseason to finish seventh
  in the Big Ten before going on to capture
  a piece of the conference's regular season title.

- And his 2006-07 UNLV Runnin' Rebels
  were projected to finish sixth in the
  Mountain West Conference prior to
  a season that saw them capture the
  attention of the nation with a Sweet 16
  appearance.

———

This is not to say these teams did not have talent. That would be unfair to say for both the players themselves as well as the coaches who assembled the teams. However, it is fair to say that all of these Kruger teams maximized their potential better than almost any other team in the country.

And maximizing one's potential is something Kruger knows about personally.

As a player at Kansas State, Kruger was the starting point guard on two Big Eight title teams, was named the Big Eight Conference Player of the Year as a junior and senior (1973 and 1974), earned Academic All-American honors as a senior and was drafted by the NBA's Atlanta Hawks. He was later voted the Big Eight Conference's All-Time "Mr. Hustle."

Surprisingly, basketball wasn't even his best — nor his favorite — sport. He also starred for the Wildcats on the baseball diamond. He had been drafted by the Houston Astros out of high school but later signed with the St. Louis Cardinals who drafted him after college. (And to make the story even more amazing, the Dallas Cowboys invited him to a tryout after his senior year in college. Kruger, who had been a star quarterback at Silver Lake High School, did not attend the workout.)

After one season pitching in the minor leagues, he played basketball for a season in Israel before heading to training camp with the NBA's Detroit Pistons. He was the last player cut by the Pistons before the season started. That's when he turned his attention to coaching.

Not a bad run for little Lonnie, all six-feet, 155-pounds of him.

———

It was August 1, 2007. None of the above accomplishments mattered to me.

Over the past few months, Coach and I had spent countless hours together talking about coaching, about leadership, about business, about relationships, about parenting — about life. I was undergoing an in-depth study on change management from one of the subject's most-qualified professors. This book project was alive and well.

But even that didn't matter to me now.

Tomorrow, Coach would be undergoing open-heart surgery, a possibility he had faced for more than 20 years because of a family history of heart problems. However, this was all so sudden.

Two nights earlier he had told me he was going in the next day for what he hoped would be a minor procedure. Something small had been detected in a routine stress test the week prior. However, "something small" turned into six bypasses.

While taking a walk alone that evening before the surgery, the reality of it all hit me. What if the worst happened? What if I lost my friend, my mentor, my coach? I stopped and silently wept.

There I stood, a better man than I was before I met him. A better father, a better husband, a better professional, a better friend, a better leader — all because of the lessons I had learned from Coach. Not Lon Kruger the basketball coach, Lon Kruger the leader of men — who just happens to be a basketball coach.

Yes, the lessons are based in simplicity. But because of the messenger and his proven past as a brilliant agent of change, those lessons have taken hold of me.

Life is not solely about winning. It's about enjoying the preparation for the fight every-day and striving to win the right way. And, throughout the entire process — even when times are tough — it's about treating all people with respect.

This book has made me a better me. For that, I am blessed.

My wish is that this book makes you a bet-ter you.

Coach just has a way of having that impact on others.

— D.J. Allen

The Simplicity of Success

Pre-game

It's simple. **Success is a process, not an event.**

That's not always the most exciting thing to hear. We want to believe in quick fixes, silver bullets, catching magic in a bottle.

But if you take the time to analyze the large majority of successful people, organizations, companies or teams, you will find that their overall success is a byproduct of simply doing the right things on a daily basis.

That is the reality we face as leaders — the simplicity of success. So how do we address something that is so elementary? How do we affirm this message with our teams day in and day out?

Welcome to the challenge of being a leader.

Game Time

The average college basketball fan would probably be surprised to learn how much our coaching staff focuses on working with players to develop them off the court, in addition to helping them improve on the court.

When these young men join our program, they are usually 18, 19 or 20 years old. Many of them are away from home for the first time.

Some arrive on the scene with a strong work ethic while some lack the concept of working hard. It is all relative to their background and surroundings. While you can learn a little something about the players during the recruiting process, there are just some things you can't find out about people until you are around them everyday.

Our objective as a staff is to develop our program for long-term success.

This means having kids on our team who are emotionally, mentally and physically able to perform at their highest level possible in basketball as well as in the classroom and socially. We want to maximize the potential of each player in our program.

In order to do this, we must start with the

basics. We talk to our kids about the simplicity of success. "Take care of what you have
to take care of today," we tell them. "If you do
this day in and day out for your entire tenure
with us, you will have success and we will
have success as a team."

It is teaching elementary principles, but it
is what works. Sound too simple? We know
it does. But the reality of our world is that our
jobs in this competitive occupational field rely
directly upon the daily decisions and habits of
fifteen 18- to 23-year-old young men.

Because of this, our primary objective is to
help our players develop habits that will make
them successful. One of the first teachings
we offer to our players is about excuses. They
need to eliminate putting themselves in a
position to have an excuse.

For example, if they are off-campus and are
leaving for class or practice, they shouldn't
plan on arriving five minutes early — they
should plan on arriving thirty minutes early.
If there are traffic problems, they will still
arrive on time if they leave earlier. There is
no excuse for not leaving earlier. "Traffic" is
simply an excuse for the real problem — a
lack of time management or laziness.

This basic way of thinking translates into
everything our players do whether it is time
management, taking care of assignments in
class or their physical conditioning.

An amazing transformation occurs once a player develops the habit of taking care of the basics on a daily basis to avoid excuses. As he witnesses the positive outcomes caused by this habit, he then begins to value the habit. More importantly, he begins to value preparation, which is what his new habit ultimately creates. This leads to the crucial development of confidence.

Confidence is the key ingredient to success. Not necessarily confidence to know you will succeed in every situation that arises, but confidence to know you have done all that you can do to prepare yourself to succeed in every situation that arises. There is a difference between the two. The first is a false sense of confidence. The second is real and life changing.

By developing good habits, players become more prepared. With that increased preparedness comes a higher level of confidence.

If we put those three things together we will win ballgames, and our players will leave our program better prepared for life. And that is how we measure success.

The Simplicity of Success

Develop Habits/Eliminate Excuses

Preparedness

Increased Sense of Confidence

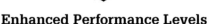

Enhanced Performance Levels

Post-game

If the proven plan for success is so simple and readily available to all of us, then why do only a select number of people and teams actually choose to follow that plan and, ultimately, decide to be successful?

Developing a plan is the easiest part — executing the plan is the challenge. A good plan doesn't offer the easiest, most convenient route. To be great at any task requires sacrifice, effort and commitment. A lack of genuine commitment to the plan is why most achieve less than their potential. If it was easy to be a champion, then all would achieve at a championship level.

If this philosophy is so basic, where and why does the breakdown occur?

What tends to happen is we don't focus enough on the tactics it takes to effectively implement a plan. It's easy to talk about the initial development of a plan as well as the desired outcomes of a plan, but the actual steps required to implement a plan correctly oftentimes go overlooked and, thus, undervalued.

Those who don't undervalue these steps are able to separate themselves from the rest of the world — whether it is in their professions or any other parts of their lives. People who choose to follow the success plan make a habit out of mastering those tactics on a daily basis. They avoid falling behind and don't need to take shortcuts or break rules to catch up.

Leaders who head successful teams make a habit out of developing productive habits for their team members. This is primarily accomplished through individual communication — on an ongoing basis — between the supervisor and team members to encourage the execution of the plan. In turn, this creates a more prepared team as well as earns the leader trust from his team as a teacher. This sense of preparedness and trust increases the team members' sense of confidence in themselves and the team, which leads to enhanced performance levels.

It's not the silver bullet theory to powerful leadership; it's just the most proven. **Ultimately, your performance as a leader is determined by how well the members of your team take care of their basic responsibilities on a daily basis.**

Sound simple? That's because it is.

The best leaders are those visionary enough to see the dream, but grounded enough to be a brilliant teacher of the basics. It's simple — don't ever stop teaching the basics.

Improve the Starting Point

Pre-game

When new coaching staffs are brought into programs — at all levels in all sports — the expectations from the stakeholders of those programs are nearly always the same: win.

While all agree on that, many times the expected time-frame for the winning to occur is not agreed upon.

Building a winning program designed for long-term success — within the rules of the NCAA — while producing student-athletes that the institution and community will be proud of ultimately means changing the existing culture, which takes time.

37

This is proven to be true in all aspects of life. However, many times stakeholders of a program think this type of talk is weak and expect results immediately in the simple terms of wins and losses.

As coaches, we expect results immediately as well. While we understand the value of the wins and losses, we know we must have other measures during this crucial building period as we are establishing the foundation on which to proceed. We focus on **improving our starting point**.

One way we work to improve our starting point is we want our team to be better at the beginning of the next season than we were at the beginning of the last season. We work to have more talented players who have better habits and are better conditioned.

The second way we strive to improve our starting point is to continue to make progress throughout the season. Teams must improve throughout the year. However, in October, we should not be working to get better for March.

Instead, we should be working to be better tomorrow. If we improve everyday in practice that means we enter the next practice or the next game at an improved starting point every time.

This theory is not always easy to grasp for someone who is not at every practice and not in every film session to see the small growth. Also, and I say this from experience, our friends in the media get bored with this type of "cliché talk."

But this philosophy brings results because it forces you to focus on improving just a little bit every single day. If you do that you will make consistent progress and eventually win games.

Game Time

We have been faced with our challenges when taking over programs at universities throughout the nation. Fortunately for us, we have surrounded ourselves with good people (who happened to be good basketball players as well) and have enjoyed successes each step along the way.

Probably the biggest rebuilding challenge we faced was when we took over at the University of Florida in 1990. Unfortunately, the program had gone through difficult times prior to us being there, and it was not just on the court.

The team finished 7–21 overall during the 1989–90 season and the program was facing heavy scrutiny and investigations by the NCAA and the FBI for off-court violations. Our directive was simple — change the culture.

After going 11–17 in our first season, we went 19–14 our second season (finishing second in our division of the SEC) while also winning three games in the NIT tournament. The next season, however, I'm sure some people thought we took a slight step backward as we went 16–12, finished third in our division and lost in the first round of the NIT.

But as coaches, we were still focused on improving the starting point during this building period. We were on the verge of creating our own culture and we could feel it.

Going into the 1993–94 season, we knew we were going to have a strong starting point to work from regardless of what our record the previous season said. The teamed gelled, worked hard every day and kept getting better each day. And that improvement ultimately showed in our wins and losses. We went on to win a then-school record 29 games and advanced to the Final Four of the NCAA Tournament.

In just four short seasons, the Gator faithful went from being ashamed by the actions of a few in its program (which almost brought the program to its knees) to enjoying the bright lights of being onstage at the Final Four.

I'm sure if you asked even the most optimistic of Gator fans they would tell you they never expected that to happen after the first three years of us being there. Had they seen improvement, yes, but the Final Four?

As coaches, however, you can't look at your program through the same lens as the fans do. You must stay focused on improving the starting point day after day, year after year.

It works. If you need proof, just look at the special young men who made up our 1993–94 Florida Gators team.

Post-game

We live in a fast-paced, results-oriented world. Because of this it can be difficult to lead.

Improvement in an organization — or even an individual — does not happen overnight. **It is a byproduct of a process**.

Because many leaders are visionary and believe they must always think in the big picture, it can become difficult for them to focus on the successes of the small improvements of their organizations. This can be dangerous as it leads to a negative frame of mind. It causes leaders — and, thus, our followers — to consistently dwell on what hasn't been accomplished instead of building upon what has been accomplished.

Are you better at what you do today than you were a year ago? Six months ago? A week ago?

How about your organization? Your individual team members?

Consistent short-term improvement leads to long-term success. It's not always about hitting the home run or focusing solely on final results.

Look for improvement in other areas daily. Are communications improving? Are we developing better client relations? Is the climate in the workplace improving?

The "simplicity of success" — leading our team to do the basic things everyday to implement our plan — contributes directly to improving the starting point.

Continually strive to improve your starting point and you can't fail.

Assertive Patience

Pre-game

Balance is life's greatest challenge.

We strive constantly to seek a healthy balance — mentally, physically and spiritually. If any one of these is not in sync, it impacts our entire whole negatively.

Our family, our friends, our profession, our faith, our charitable work, our health — these responsibilities require us to work at maintaining a level of balance in our lives on a daily basis.

Like life itself, being a strong leader is about balance and **often that search for balance leads us to a paradox**. This is the case when practicing the art of assertive patience.

Game Time

Our world keeps telling us to value getting our information faster and easier. Not necessarily to get it more accurately, but to get it as soon as possible. That includes scrolls on TV, Blackberries, chat rooms and message boards.

We are being conditioned to want more and to want it now — in almost every aspect of our lives. Incredible advancements in technology, of course, are leading us in this direction. But while technology is developing rapidly, human nature remains consistent.

This ultimately leads us to a battle leaders face everyday. How do you stay patient and committed to your long-term goals in an increasingly impatient world?

We face this predicament on an on-going basis as college coaches. Our staff's number one priority must be to develop a basketball program that will be successful over a long period of time. However, in an industry where many people want to believe you are only as good as the score of your last game, it is easy to feel conflicted.

This is why, as leaders of the program, we must practice assertive patience.

"Assertive" meaning that, on a daily basis, we are teaching the tactics that will make us a successful program. We must continually hold everyone within our program accountable for their actions.

Day in and day out we must provide our players with constant feedback, praise, and direction in an effort to maximize each of their individual potential. This will ultimately allow us to maximize our team's potential.

We must set expectations and measure them everyday. This effort by our coaches must be non-stop. It must be relentless.

Now for the challenging part — the paradox. **While being obsessively assertive with the daily tactics, we must have the "patience" to allow the processes to work**.

People will fail at times. Teams will fail at times. It is human nature. Improvement and forward movement is made by taking baby steps, not giant leaps. We must expect failure and not allow ourselves to get frustrated by it. Getting frustrated will only lead to us not doing what we are supposed to be doing. That is, reinforcing the execution of the plan, individually and as a team, on a daily basis.

Learning is a process and we have to appreciate this. Our job is to make sure there is continual progression from our team even if the most tangible outcomes — the scores — are not always positive.

This concept can be a difficult one to accept for many coaches, especially many young assistant coaches. It is not uncommon for teams to take two steps forward and then one step back. You have to be comfortable with this reality and how to address it so the team continues to make strides.

We practice assertive patience in many different forms — both short and long-term as well as with individuals and teams.

During individual games, there are times we must stay patient that a game plan will work even if we start off slowly. It's critical that we be assertive in accomplishing the tactics yet stay patient so that we will receive the desired outcomes.

In individual seasons, we must practice assertive patience with the team as well as individual players. A player may start out the season struggling, but that is not reason for us to give up on him. On a daily basis we need to be assertive that he is doing what needs to be done — extra shooting, additional conditioning, etc. If he is doing all that we ask of him, chances are he will begin to play at a higher level. We just have to have the patience to allow the process to work, as well as give him positive praise for his effort and remind him about the potential outcomes of the process.

And of course, we must practice assertive patience through the development of our program. This may be the most difficult of all for coaches in any sport.

Followers of any team at any level want to enjoy success. Understandably, they would much rather enjoy it sooner than later. However, when building a program, what might help you win immediately is not always what is best for building a success-ful program for the long-term. Coaches are constantly faced with decisions that may hurt them immediately, but help them in the long run.

Adding to this mix is the reality that most followers of a program are not in a position to witness the assertiveness on a daily basis as well as the smaller progres-sions. Thus, when coaches preach patience to allow the process to work, there may be a disconnect with some supporters of the program.

This adds more of a burden on coaches to remain patient while allowing the pro-cesses to work. Outside pressure must not influence a coaching staff's actions in such a way that it negatively impacts their team.

Our experiences at Florida and UNLV have been similar in the fact that our break-through seasons came unexpectedly to people outside the programs, but not to the players and coaches.

We advanced to the Final Four with Florida in 1994 — our fourth season with the Gators — a year removed from a 16–12 season and a first-round loss in the NIT. Prior to the 1993–94 season we had been picked to finish eighth overall in the SEC.

Needless to say, many people were surprised by our 29–8 season that left us one game away from playing for a national title.

During our third season at UNLV in 2006–07, we finished 30–7 and made it to the Sweet 16. We finished the season ranked number 14 in the nation, even though we were picked to finish just sixth in the Mountain West Conference prior to the campaign.

In both instances, we were assertive about what had to happen on a daily basis for us to begin to build the programs we inherited into top caliber programs. Internally, we were confident the processes would work in a matter of a few years. We improved daily and saw the breakthrough seasons coming.

Externally, however, most did not anticipate the breakthroughs. The improvement was not as evident and as immediate as many now want it to be.

Despite this fact, we never wavered. We would rather have the patience to stick to an accurate plan than take shortcuts that will hurt us in the long run.

This is one of the challenges NBA franchises face. The structure of the league is set in a way that it takes a longer period of time to change a losing culture into a winning culture. However, due to a lack of patience, many coaching and management changes are made during the early stages of a culture alteration. That ultimately leads to a cycle of failure for those organizations constantly in a state of change.

Post-game

Many people often mistake patience for passiveness. It can be viewed as a weakness or a lack of passion, particularly in our ever-changing world when results are expected immediately.

Leaders must be secure enough to remain patient to allow processes to work. A leader can feel comfortable in this patience if he is confident the tactics to achieve his team's success are being assertively addressed on a daily basis.

Breakdowns in this process will occur due to a lack of short-term objectives being identified for team members. (These short-term objectives, of course, must be aligned with the team's overall long-term goals.) Clear expectations must be set for team members and we — as leaders — are responsible for providing team members with constant feedback, praise and direction.

Without this assertive effort to manage daily expectations, the long-term success of the team will be jeopardized. Ultimately, we as leaders will be held responsible for the failure.

Practicing assertive patience is also crucial

49

when it comes to building a team. The first thing a successful leader does is make sure employees are in the correct positions to succeed. Leaders must identify team members who fit and put them into roles where they can achieve. After doing this, he or she must give the process time to work as the team members adapt to their new roles.

Some people like to claim they are big picture thinkers and value the long-term more. Others say they would rather see immediate results and put more value in short-term achievement.

True leaders recognize, appreciate and are able to actively address both. The best leaders seek balance. They are assertive as well as patient.

Focus on Performance — Not Promotion

Pre-game

Success is not easy to come by. However, the strategy to be successful is not complicated.

So many of us want the next raise, the next big thing we can buy with that raise or, better yet, the next promotion. It is easy for that to become our focus.

Yet the only way to obtain these is to perform on a daily basis. This is not always attractive and certainly not easy for many of us to stay focused on. However, performing at a high-level on a daily basis is the key to moving forward in anything.

Focus on performance — not promotion. And with a little patience and solid performance, you will find great rewards.

Game Time

Entering our third season at UNLV, we were selected to finish sixth in the Mountain West Conference.

We had a core group of unheralded seniors we were going to rely upon.

Guard Michael Umeh was returning for his fourth season with the team and was coming off a season where he had struggled with knee problems.

My son, Kevin, was joining the team as point guard for his senior season after playing at Arizona State for three years.

Wendell White, who played guard/forward, was playing his second season after transferring from junior college. Although he was an important recruit for us the season before, a broken foot slowed him and he underperformed his junior year.

We also had two senior centers who had come to us via the junior college ranks — Joel Anthony and Gaston Essengue. Both had potential, but neither one of them had proven themselves in games during their short careers with us.

Although the fans and media did not

expect much from the team, we believed we had a chance to surprise a lot of people with the performance of our five leaders.

Throw in our talented sophomore guard Wink Adams and we had six players who on any given night could carry our team to victory.

While that was definitely an asset, it could have also been a large liability.

All five seniors believed in their hearts that they had a chance to continue their playing careers after college and wanted a chance to prove themselves to scouts during the season. (I'm sure most people outside of our locker room would have laughed at that notion prior to the season, but it was a reality from the outset.)

And complicating matters further was the fact Adams, the sophomore, was probably the most gifted player of the bunch and was ready to blossom into one of the top players on the West Coast.

So the question loomed — was any one player going to put his interest in promotion over his interest in performance? Unfortunately, in a team setting, all it takes is for one player to do this and the entire team suffers.

Fortunately for us, our team acted as just that — a team. And each day our guys worked on performing better, both as individuals and as a team.

While White led us in scoring 13 times

and rebounding 17 times that season, he had help from a balanced attack. Adams led us in scoring in 12 games and Kevin led us nine times, including in six of our last nine games of the season. Umeh peaked at the right time, leading us in scoring during our conference tournament championship win over BYU as well as our first round NCAA Tournament victory over Georgia Tech and our Sweet 16 loss to Oregon.

On the boards, Anthony and Essengue both led the way in nine games each and both played aggressive defense in the middle throughout the year.

The team, which was picked to finish only sixth in the nine team conference wound up 30–7 overall, won the conference tournament championship, and made it all the way to the Sweet 16. In fact, we finished ranked number 14 in the nation in the final Coaches Top 25 poll of the season.

Why? Because our players made a conscious decision to focus on performance, not promotion.

But an ironic thing happened. **By focusing on performance and winning as a team our player's were given the opportunity for personal promotion**. The following season, all five seniors continued their playing careers at the professional level.

Anthony, who despite coming off the

bench for us during his senior year, was named the Mountain West Conference's Defensive Player of the Year and spent the next season playing for the NBA's Miami Heat.

Kevin, who won MVP honors for the Mountain West Conference Tournament, was invited to veteran training camp by the Orlando Magic and was the final player to be let go before the season started. He continued his career in the NBA's Development League as did White, who was named our team's MVP in a close vote.

Essengue and Umeh signed to play in Europe the following season and Adams, the only non-senior, was named second-team All-Mountain West Conference that season and was a preseason first team All-MWC pick prior to his junior year.

Each player ultimately received his personal promotion, but only because he concentrated not only on his own personal performance but also his team's performance.

Post-game

One of the best characteristics of leaders, particularly young leaders, is their aggressiveness and assertiveness. They work hard and have high expectations for themselves.

However, it is also very easy for these types of individuals to begin to focus their efforts on the wrong things — the next promotion or the next big break. This lack of focus can lead to a breakdown in performance and, ultimately, cost someone an opportunity for a better position.

This is where the practice of "assertive patience" is so critical. This means being "assertive" on a day-to-day basis regarding what needs to be done today to make you and your team better tomorrow. This includes understanding daily expectations, providing and gaining feedback daily and simply working harder than anyone to get better at whatever it is you do. Consistency is the most important trait in this effort as you focus on your performance — and what you can control — on a daily basis.

The paradox, of course, is the "patience" aspect of this philosophy. You have to believe in the process of your daily "assertiveness" and allow ample time for the process to work. The houses true leaders live in are not made of cards — you cannot pull out one card and have the entire house crumble to the ground.

It takes time and dedication to build a solid foundation as a leader. If you are good at what you do and you perform well and help your team to perform well, you will achieve the next promotion or the next opportunity. However, don't allow yourself to focus on the promotion. Always focus on performance.

Compete for Results

Pre-game

It is not enough to simply say we want our players to compete hard.

That is too vague. There needs to be something gained out of that effort, something tangible.

While obviously a win is tangible, that is still not the proper metric by which we measure how a player or our team is competing. A win, in fact, is a byproduct of other successes. A win in itself is not a success. Instead, it represents a multitude of successes during a particular contest.

We want our players to compete for

results. If they compete for results and achieve those desired results, more often than not, we will win.

Game Time

Competing for results starts in the practice gym.

Good teams get after it in practice. Players go nose-to-nose competing for playing time. All the while everyone is helping everyone else raise the level of their respective games.

During practice drills, the desired outcome has nothing to do with a scoreboard, thus, the score cannot be used as a metric. We want our players to embrace this and focus on more identifiable and more immediate results.

Compete for the strong block out. *Compete* to set the proper screen. *Compete* to finish the shot. Players have control over these outcomes by how they compete for the desired results.

Our job as coaches is to ensure this "competing for results" carries over into games. Whether we are up by ten points or down by ten, we must always stay focused on competing for results. We want our players to play every possession like it's the last possession of the game and will determine the result. We want this to become a habit.

Competing to win each possession means we must always focus on the details. We never talk about simply winning with our team. We do talk about doing all of the little things well and that will give us the best chance to win, regardless of the score.

Once your team begins competing based upon the score, you will find slippage within the details and fundamentals.

That happened to our 2006–07 UNLV team one winter Saturday afternoon in Provo, Utah, playing a red-hot BYU team that was riding a 27-game home winning streak. We had entered the game with a five-game winning streak and had been ranked number 25 in the nation the previous Monday — the first time in 15 years UNLV had been nationally ranked.

We fought to stay within two points eight minutes into the game before BYU exploded from beyond the arc. The Cougars went on a 23–8 run with a barrage of three-pointers and we never recovered.

As soon as we found ourselves down by double digits, we stopped competing for results and started competing based upon the score. We played desperate, and not the good kind. A school-record 15 BYU three-pointers later, we headed home having lost by 27 points.

We were crushed at the time. But little did we know that experience would help us win a conference tournament championship just six weeks later.

In the championship game of the Mountain West Conference tournament, we got one more crack at the Cougars, who had worked their way into the Top 25 and came into the game with a load of momentum. And it showed from the tip-off.

BYU continued where it had left off against us and knocked us to the canvas early with a 16–3 run to start the game. We struggled to keep the Cougars within striking distance and still found ourselves down by as many as 13 with less than a half of the basketball game remaining.

So there we were with our NCAA Tournament hopes on the line and facing a team that had absolutely dominated us the last 60-plus minutes we had played them. There was only one thing left for us to do — compete for results.

And that is exactly what our guys did. They competed to box out and secured the rebounds. They competed to set screens and got the shooter open. They competed to finish the shot . . . and they did. They weren't competing for the score, they were simply competing for results one play at a time.

We had tried to do it the other way six weeks earlier and were utterly controlled. This time, we were going to control the things we could control.

Little by little we chipped away at the big margin and took our first lead of the game, 51–50, with 11:45 to go. The lead would change hands six times over the next six minutes before our senior guard Michael Umeh — who led us with 18 points that evening — put us ahead for good with 5:33 left en route to a 78–70 win.

For three seasons at UNLV we had emphasized competing for results with our players. On that night our success in competing for results gained our team and our fans a conference title and an automatic bid to the Big Dance.

Our Kansas State squad had faced a similar situation almost 20 years earlier. During our run to the Elite Eight in 1988, we were able to knock off number one-seeded Purdue, 73–70, in the NCAA Tournament despite falling to the Boilermakers by 29 points in a game earlier that season.

We won because we didn't focus on winning the rematch. We simply focused on competing for results.

Post-game

What are the results team members in your organization should be competing for on a day-to-day basis?

Vague phrases such as "superior customer service" or "increased revenues" are not enough for our followers to concentrate on daily. These are the byproducts of other successes.

Figure out what leads to these outcomes and how to best measure that. For "superior customer service," is it how quickly a phone call or e-mail is returned, or how flawless your billing system is operating? For "increased revenues" is it the amount of leads generated or does it have something to do with billing more aggressively?

Rolling the ball out to mid-court and telling your team to "Go, play hard and win" is not enough. **Leaders must set expectations for their team members to strive for on a daily basis**.

What realistically can your team members work on to accomplish *today* that will ultimately help your organization meet its long-term goals?

If you have correctly communicated this to your followers and you continually reinforce this plan, you are appropriately leading your team to compete for results.

Living Life Backwards

Pre-game

What if you could live your life backwards? Backwards in a way that you would see the consequences of your actions before actually committing those acts. Are there things you would change? I know in my life there are.

Obviously, this is only a hypothetical question. However, it is not hypothetical to think in this manner. Some people see this as a type of "feed-forward" process. "Feed-forward" meaning you have the ability to anticipate feedback from your actions before making those acts. Thus, with careful thought, this allows you to alter your actions as needed to give you the desired best outcomes.

It's a way of looking ahead, **of realizing there are consequences — intended and unintended — for every action or lack of action**.

This is what the Xs and Os of basketball are about. If the offense does this, the defense has options to do that. We are picturing the results of our possible actions and determining which specific actions — that we can control — will best lead us to our objective.

Game Time

There is a feeling much worse than being eliminated from tournament play come March or April. That is having the feeling that you know you could have done things differently from September through March that would have led to better success for your team's just concluded season.

As coaches we do everything we can to avoid this feeling. It is unacceptable.

Sports allow you to enjoy new life and new beginnings. With each new season comes a renewed hope of a championship campaign.

This also allows you the opportunity to reflect upon what works and what doesn't work with your teams. Each year you build upon that until you find a formula that works for your teams during the long seasons. You work to have your team continuing to make strides in an effort to peak at the right time — during post-season play.

Sometimes it works. Sometimes it does not. Sometimes the coach of a Sweet 16 team walks away more fulfilled than the coach of a Final Four team whose team lost in the national semifinals. It all depends whether either team could have done anything differently to better maximize its potential. If the Sweet 16 team was picked to finish in the middle of the pack of its own conference and was not even expected to make the tournament, while the Final Four team was considered the most-talented team in the land, then, which team did the most with its talent? The Sweet 16 team.

Our goal at the end of the season — no matter the outcome — is to have no questions lingering about what we could have controlled over the past six months. The only way to do this, however, is to start acting upon this in September when workouts start.

Come the end of the season, we cannot be thinking, "If only. . . ?" There are no "if onlys," there are no do-overs. To be prepared for March we must be taking care of our responsibilities in September. Each day is significant. Each day must bring with it its own sense of urgency about what has to be accomplished that day for us to win.

What can we do today that will make us better tomorrow? That must be our mindset each and every day, both on the court and off the court.

We must continually remind our players about the consequences of their actions whether it is how they perform during a practice in mid-November or how they act at a party on a Saturday night in February. Each event will play a role in how we perform as a team when March comes around.

College basketball fans, coaches and players love to say they live for March. But that is not enough for the members of our team. We must live everyday with March in mind.

That way we don't end up living with questions lingering after the season is over.

Post-game

What is the goal your team is being challenged to meet? Start at what that goal is and work backwards. What has to occur for your team to ultimately meet that goal? Work all the way backwards until you reach today. Now ask yourself, "What do you have to do today to make sure you are working towards the final goal? Then, what do I have to do tomorrow?"

Begin to look at the processes by which you are trying to meet goals as a season. Right now is training camp and everyday you are one step closer to playing in the post-season and playing to achieve your goal.

It's hard for your team members to stay this focused each and every day. That is your job as their leader guiding them through change. You must continually remind them of what needs to be accomplished daily and keep them on track.

Analyze your team's results periodically and relate them to your long-term goals. This allows you to have ever-changing standards to help raise the bar, which is a key element to changing a culture. However, be sure not to celebrate too early. Celebrate when achievements are accomplished, but quickly refocus.

It is important to learn to anticipate the consequences of your actions as well as your team's actions. Then, be sure you are able to illustrate to your team the consequences — intended and unintended — caused by the actions or lack of actions. This is a constant and on-going process during which you must highlight the positives as well as constructively address the negatives.

When addressing the negatives and critiquing employees, we need to do it in a way that best affects performance. This is done by anticipating an employee's reaction to the criticism and, thus, communicating with him in a way that will benefit the team in the long run.

We cannot live our lives backwards. However, as leaders, we must practice "feed-forward" tactics to anticipate consequences of our actions and address them before they occur.

Some people think effective leaders are good at anticipating future outcomes. In actuality, **effective leaders are good at *creating* future outcomes**.

An Underdog's Margin of Error

Pre-game

Your concentration level heightens **when you are aware you have no or very little margin for error**. Performing with this increased focus often allows you to produce better results.

Thus, rather than focusing directly on results, identify what will allow you and your team to perform with an increased level of focus.

Game Time

As a player at Kansas State University, scrimmaging in practice was one of my favorite things to do. And nothing motivated me more than to size up the two teams the coaches selected and see that the team I was on was considered the underdog.

There is no margin for error when you are the underdog. You must play with an increased sense of focus and treat every possession with significance. Underdog teams cannot make mistakes and still have a chance of winning.

I used to love playing with this healthy pressure. Winning when perceived as the underdog is so much more satisfying.

As coaches, our programs have always been designed with this mindset.

Treating each possession with significance is at the core of everything we do. When our teams are playing at their highest levels, we will not beat ourselves.

Whether we are the underdog on paper or not is irrelevant to us. We want our players to play with this mindset because this creates the habit of playing with the highest level of focus at all times.

Upsets occur when the team favored to win loses focus, while the underdog team stays focused on the details and builds its confidence as it enjoys success

throughout the game. If both teams maximize their potential, obviously the favorite will win. However, rarely do both teams play to their maximum potential in the same game.

And because there is so much parity these days in the college ranks, the team that comes closest to maximizing its potential will usually come out on top. Thus, our objective is to maximize our team's potential in each and every game, and the underdog mentality allows us to increase our focus. This underdog mentality has been a big factor during our most successful seasons

We took over the Florida Gators program in the summer of 1990. The team was coming off of a 7–21 season, but more disappointing to the Gator faithful, the program was being investigated by both the NCAA and FBI for off-court violations.

During our first year in Gainesville, we began to work on changing the culture of the program and finished the season with an 11–17 mark. We made big strides our second season and advanced all the way to the semifinals of the NIT post-season tournament. Our record of 19–14, a second place finish in the SEC's Eastern Division and our post-season run raised expectations for our third year.

That season, however, we finished third in the division and returned to the NIT. This time we lost in the first round and ended the year with a mark of 16–12.

We had obviously improved the starting point of the program from when we first took over. But neither the media nor the fans had high expectations for our 1993–94 group. Our schedule featured 11 games against teams that had played in the NCAA Tournament the previous March.

The preseason prognosis was for us to finish fourth in the SEC's Eastern Division and eighth overall. And that was fine by us. We relished being in the role of underdog.

Led by our emotional leader, senior guard Craig Brown, we played the entire season with the confidence of champions, but also the focus of underdogs.

After our first 20 games, we were 17–3, which was the best start in the school's 75-year basketball history. Six games later, we advanced to 22–4 with a win over in-state rival Florida State, and were ranked number 16 in the nation. The 22 wins set a new school record for regular season victories, and we were not done yet.

We finished first in the SEC's Eastern Division before falling to a Rick Pitino-coached Kentucky squad in the finals of the SEC Tournament.

On Selection Sunday, we gathered in front of the television waiting to be officially invited to the NCAA Tournament — something very few, if any, outside of our locker room thought would be possible some four months earlier.

Not only were we invited, our accomplishments were recognized with a number 3 seed in the East Regional. After beating James Madison and Penn in the first two rounds to advance to the Sweet 16, we headed to Miami to face number 2-seeded Connecticut.

The *Miami Herald* greeted us with a headline that reinforced our position: "No Fear: Underdog's Here." Our guys delivered again as we upset Donyell Marshall and the rest of the Jim Calhoun-led Huskies in overtime, 69–60.

At this point in the season our players' focus was almost unshakeable as they dearly embraced the underdog role. But little did we know that would be challenged.

Boston College was the new Cinderella at our dance. The eighth-seeded Golden Eagles had already disposed of number one seed North Carolina and followed that up with another upset of Indiana to advance to the Elite Eight and a matchup with us.

No longer were we the true underdogs. However, our guys kept their focus. We trailed 56–53 with five minutes left to play before Brown took the game over and helped lead us to a 74–66 victory and the unthinkable — a trip to the Final Four.

It was the first Final Four appearance in school history and we were matched up in the national semifinal game against Grant Hill and the rest of Mike Krzyzewski's Duke Blue Devils, who were playing in their seventh Final Four in nine years.

Our group of underdogs fought their way out to a 13-point lead early in the second half before Hill took over. He sparked a Duke run to get his team back in the game. Brown's jumper gave us the lead, 63–62, at the 2:32 mark, but that would be the last time we would have a lead. Final score: Duke 70, Florida 65.

We did not return home champions in the eyes of the entire basketball world. But we were champions in the eyes of our fans and of those who didn't believe in us back in November.

Our players embraced the underdog mentality and never let their focus slip. They played 37 games with very little margin for error that season and walked off the floor 29 times as the winner. They simply found a way.

Post-game

The most successful teams are the teams who have the top talent available, the confidence of a champion and the focus of an underdog.

For many reasons, however, these teams rarely exist.

It is obvious that not every team will have the top talent available — in fact, most teams will not. And, of course, without producing any results, having the confidence of a champion can be difficult.

However, **there is one thing all teams should work to obtain — performing with the focus of an underdog**. Unmatched focus can overcome many obstacles, including a lack of talent, and allow performance at the highest level possible.

The top leaders have a knack for keeping their teams hungry, keeping their teams focused on what needs to be done each and every day to achieve overall success. They focus on every possession, every detail and give nothing away.

When you are the underdog in sports or in business, there is no margin for error. To win, you must take advantage of every opportunity that presents itself to you. Without focus, this is not possible.

Eventually, however, this increased focus will help to produce results, which will lead to the opportunity for your team to have the confidence of a champion. And finally, it will help lead your team to attracting the best talent available.

It is important at this point not to forget where you and your team started — as the underdog. No matter what talent you have, or what confidence you have, compete as though you are the underdog. Compete as though you have no margin for error. This type of focus is unmatched.

The Winning Season Formula

Pre-game

Most spectators only measure success in sports by the big picture. They measure by league and division championships, major titles in sports like golf and tennis, and overall post-season success.

If our teams only measure success in this same way, then we are not doing our job as coaches. Our job consists of laying out a plan that, when implemented, leads to the big picture success of realizing potential.

That plan must include intermediate goals and objectives that are tangible. Seasons are too long and consist of too many variables to rely simply upon the season's overall outcome to keep players focused and moving in the same direction.

When you break a season down game by game, you soon understand **there is a formula to a winning season**.

First, you win the games you are supposed to win. Second, you win a majority of the games that are considered toss-ups. Finally, you surprise everyone by pulling off one or two upsets.

If you do this, the big picture success of the season will take care of itself.

Game Time

Our 2006–07 UNLV squad that advanced to the Sweet 16 was our first team to reach the 30 win mark (30–7). In a number of ways the accomplishments of this team were as fulfilling to our staff as any other teams' accomplishments throughout our careers.

We started the season encouraged by the off-season workouts. Being picked to finished sixth in our conference gave us the opportunity to surprise a lot of people.

Looking at the schedule, we felt if we could

follow the "winning formula" and win the games we were supposed to win, we could pick up a greater number of toss-up wins and upset wins than most were expecting.

However, we had a challenge early in the season. We ran into a hot-shooting UC Santa Barbara team in our third game of the season and, playing without our injured starting point guard, Kevin Kruger (which would become a reoccurring theme, unfortunately) we suffered a three-point defeat at home.

Those losses hurt. It was a game we were supposed to win and, if you look at our track record, rarely do our teams get upset. We like to think this is because we make a great effort to get our guys to focus on the details and execute the fundamentals on each possession no matter who the opponent is.

So instead of being 5–0 when we traveled to play Arizona in Tucson, we were a little disappointed to be 4–1. Against Arizona, we held the lead most of the first half, but the nationally ranked Wildcats were too much for us and we were not able to pull off the upset. That put us at 4–2 with an interesting stretch of games in front of us.

Back in Las Vegas, the fans were a little restless. It was our third season at UNLV, and despite us knowing the talent level of players had been raised and that we were improving the culture inside the program, the results were not yet evident to the public.

For us to get to where we wanted to be, we were going to have to win a few toss-up games as well as pull off an upset or two. And that is exactly what we did.

We put everything together in a 40-point win over Northern Arizona in a neutral site game. The Lumberjacks had upset UNLV at the Thomas & Mack Center the year prior to us arriving in Las Vegas.

Then it was time for a difficult two-game road swing to Hawaii, which beats about 80 percent of its non-conference visitors, and to Reno, where the nationally-ranked Wolf Pack of the University of Nevada–Reno always wants a piece of its in-state rival from the South.

We won in Hawaii with a late jumper by Wendell White before heading up to Reno where most thought we would be lucky if we held the game to within single-digits. Instead, we jumped out to a 19-point first half lead and went on to win, 58–49, for UNLV's first road win over a nationally-ranked team in 15 years.

Just more than three weeks after the disappointing loss on our home court to Santa Barbara, we were now back on track by winning a toss-up game and notching two upset victories on the road.

We stretched our winning streak to seven with four victories at home prior to Christmas

— including wins over Minnesota out of the Big Ten and Texas A&M–Corpus Christi, which would later qualify for the NCAA Tournament — before hitting the road to experience something our guys had never expected. We were visiting Texas Tech, and the nation's eyes would be focused on the game because head coach Bobby Knight would be attempting to become the all-time winningest coach in college basketball history that night.

In a pure basketball sense, our upset win at Reno was bigger. But from a national perspective, our 74–66 win at Texas Tech on national television got the attention of college basketball followers across the nation.

We concluded non-conference play that year with a 13–2 mark, probably a few games better than even the most optimistic of fans expected. We then went 12–4 during conference play, which was UNLV's best regular season ever in Mountain West Conference play. It included an 8–0 mark at home even though we played both BYU and San Diego State with key starters injured.

All four of the losses on the road in conference play came at the hands of the other top four teams in the league, meaning we won the games against the bottom teams . . . the games we were supposed to win.

We then won three games to capture the Mountain West Conference Tournament championship before beating Georgia Tech in the first round of the NCAA Tournament. We followed that up by knocking off the number two seed, Wisconsin, to advance to the Sweet 16, where Oregon would eventually eliminate us.

Many fans will remember the 2006–07 season for our big wins at Reno and Texas Tech as well as our post-season wins over BYU, Georgia Tech and, of course, Wisconsin. And rightfully so.

But what made this team so special was that it always took care of business when it needed to and won the games it was supposed to win, even when the eyes of the nation were not looking at them. We finished with a 19–1 mark at home that season winning the final 17 games at the Thomas & Mack, a sign of a strong program.

We won the games we were supposed to win. We won a majority of the toss-up games. And, of course, we enjoyed our fair share of upsets.

Post-game

Everyone loves the big win. Whether it's an upset win in sports, or the big new contract in business.

But success is not made off of the big win. Success is built of making a habit of winning consistently, even at a smaller level. That prepares and puts your team in position for the big win.

The winning season formula can be utilized in business through the *"Raise, Retain and Recruit Method."*

Raise your clients. The greatest area for immediate revenue growth in a company is to raise its current clientele/customers to the highest level they should attain. This involves servicing them at a high level and continually educating them on the value you can offer. Many times, particularly in the ever-growing professional services sector, we are so happy to just have someone as a client that we don't maximize their potential. These should be easy wins.

Retain your clients. Once you have raised your clients to the levels at which they should be providing revenue, you need to work at retaining them. Obviously, losing a profitable client has a large negative impact on your organization. Make clients feel appreciated and respected and you will retain a large majority of these crucial clients. Don't take them for granted. These wins — or losses — can make or break your season. Strive to find the balance of working to retain clients while recruiting new ones.

Recruit new clients. This is the big upset. You cannot focus on this at all times although many people do. It is attractive, yet it can be dangerous. If you are spending too much time looking for the big win, chances are you are not raising your current clients or spending the time to retain your clients. New clients will come if current clients are happy.

Success is in the day-to-day details. To win big, you have to think small.

That is small with regard to taking care of the details and fundamentals each day.

Quiet Confidence

Pre-game

Ego is a misunderstood thing.

Successful leaders have bigger egos than most other people. However, **they are successful at leading others because they are better at suppressing their egos publicly than most.**

This is possible because of the strong confidence they possess in themselves. Their confidence not only allows them to believe they will accomplish what they are charged with, it also allows them to believe they will receive the due credit and recognition without actively seeking it.

Negative consequences from enlarged egos occur when people are not confident they will receive the accolades they believe are necessary. If this is the case, a big ego, which should be an asset, turns into a rather large liability for all involved.

Security is a crucial trait, particularly for agents of change. Without it, failure looms.

Game Time

It's somewhat flattering to hear some say that my wife Barb and I don't have big egos, but the people who say that couldn't be more wrong.

We have worked hard and are fortunate to have been blessed with, and enjoy, the life-style that we live. Both of us are very proud of our successes on the court and in the communities in which we have lived and been active. Thus, we work hard to protect our names. That is called having an ego the last time I checked.

Dad taught all of us growing up that humility is one of the most important traits a person could have. At the same time, he taught us to have confidence in whatever it was that we were doing. Basically, Dad taught us to have "quiet confidence." **He would say, "Never talk about yourself. If you do something well enough, others will speak for your accomplishments."**

To this day, I am very confident in myself, in my abilities, and the abilities of those people around me. We take great pride (there's that ego again) in producing winning teams and graduating players. Without an ego, this would not be as important.

However, it has never been my style — nor will it ever be my style — to go on a tirade in the media to try to explain just how much I want to win. In the past, some have criticized me for this. However, words are just that — words. Dad taught us to take action if we wanted to achieve something and that is where we focus our energy.

Barb and I are very confident in the way we live our lives. We want our names to be associated with good, and work hard to insure this. In fact, because of our positions, every time we are in public — whether it is related to basketball or not — we are on display and we are very aware of this. Our actions have consequences that impact our program, our institution, our community, and us. We take this responsibility very seriously.

The danger is when we stop taking the *responsibility* seriously and start taking *ourselves* too seriously. We are still the same two kids who grew up in small towns in

Kansas, fell in love in college, and chased a dream together. We have helped one another to try and keep a level head through all of our journeys and successes — and failures — throughout the years.

Looking back on our experiences, the most amazing thing about all of the professional and financial success is that we never sought it. We always strived to simply succeed by doing things we felt was the right way and the rest found us.

I now have a greater appreciation for what Dad taught us all those years ago about confidence. You must have the right amount of confidence to succeed. Without it, you will fail at whatever it is you are trying to accomplish.

At the same time, you must have even more confidence to remain humble. This confidence allows you to understand that you will eventually receive all of the deserved accolades and benefits even though you do not publicly seek it.

Publicly seeking these accolades — or having "loud confidence" — actually displays a person's insecurities.

Stay humble. Stay patient. Stay confident. And success will follow.

Post-game

Successful leaders want to build teams featuring people with large egos. This insures that team members will take pride in the results of their work.

The key to managing these types of individuals, however, is to create an environment, which encourages teammates to publicly suppress their egos. Providing positive feedback and recognition to those deserving it — without them publicly seeking it — can create this type of environment. In fact, publicly seeking accolades should be frowned upon in the team setting.

This all starts with you — the leader. Are you secure enough not to publicly seek recognition and accolades? Are you confident enough to surround yourself with strong teammates and not be intimidated by it?

Don't mistake "loud confidence" as being a greater sign of confidence when, in fact, it generally exposes individuals for their lack of self-confidence.

The most secure leaders — and their top teammates — are the ones who are quietly confident. They know how to get results and are confident they will be rewarded for their performances. This is the highest level of confidence there is.

Healthy Pressure

Pre-game

Pressure is a good thing when used correctly. It can increase focus while bringing people together.

The more you can control the pressure in an environment, the more of an ally pressure becomes.

Operating without any pressure can be detrimental to a team. Not only is the team not challenged to be focused, when the time comes for the team to face adversarial pressure, chances are the team will not be as prepared as possible.

Game Time

There is no way to simulate true game pressure for athletes.

That being said, our job as coaches is to prepare our teams for game pressure as much as possible by constantly having them perform in practice under healthy pressure situations.

We are able to accomplish this through drills that we run in practice. Basically anything you need to work on as a team can be converted into a drill. We like to add pressure to many of our drills by adding the element of time.

Through the use of the clock, we measure the effectiveness of the team during the drills by keeping score and pitting the team against itself and previous scores from the same drill.

Athletes are competitive by nature. By making drills a competition, it not only makes the practice more enjoyable for our players — rather than feeling like they are just going through the motions — it also helps us to come together closer as a team.

The area that is most positively impacted by practicing in healthy pressure situations is focus. A timed drill may be as simple as a fast-break lay-up drill with no one contesting the shot. One missed shot during this drill can cause the team not to score at the level that is expected. We find that players, not wanting to let their teammates down, perform the drill with an increased level of focus. Our goal then is to for them to emulate this type of focus at all times.

What we are ultimately seeking from our players is the ability to perform with the highest level of concentration from start to finish during games. This is only possible if our players learn to play every single possession — both offensively and defensively — as if it were the last possession of the game and the outcome depends upon this possession.

That expectation of our team puts our players in a pressure situation every time they are on the court. We, however, believe this expectation produces healthy pressure.

If, in fact, our players take ownership of this belief and focus on each and every possession with the same importance of a final possession, they will be ready for the challenge at the end of the game when one possession truly will decide the winner.

More importantly, this type of focus for an entire game will put us in a position to win the game without having it come down to a final possession.

What a team must always try to avoid is giving away possessions — both on offense and on defense. This occurs from a lack of focus, sometimes by just one person on the team.

Every possession of every game and practice matters. Our players know this is our expectation and they play under that healthy pressure every game and every practice.

Post-game

The next time one of your teammates is going to meet with a client, ask him, "Is this a sales meeting?"

A typical response may be, "Nope. We're just meeting to go over a few things."

Your response, **"Remember, it's always a sales meeting."**

Help the members of your team to understand the importance of each and every responsibility that they have and the relationships they possess. If we are dealing with people in any way — even if we are not in sales — we need to be focused on our objectives at all times, or we risk losing something valuable. This is true for every phone call, every meeting, and every email.

Team members need to feel the healthy pressure of being responsible for the success of your team. This accountability helps them to focus on their work as well as to feel valued.

Don't fall into the trap of believing you're being a good leader because you have alleviated all of the pressure from your team. All teams need to operate under healthy pressure. Without it, they are being set up for eventual failure.

Celebrate Consistency

Pre-game

We rarely celebrate consistency. However, when consistency in our lives is not present, we yearn for it.

There are too many variables in all aspects of life to expect life itself to be consistent, and this is true in the world of sports as well. During tough times is when a leader must rise to the occasion, to offer a steadying hand and guide his team through the challenging periods.

A successful leader is a consistent leader. You know what to expect from the leader during the good times and the bad times — at all times. With this leadership, good teams can grow stronger during both success and adversity and evolve into championship teams.

Game Time

No matter the sport, teams look good when things are going well. During a winning streak, a team's weaknesses will appear less vulnerable than before, while its strengths may seem stronger than they actually are.

The true measure of a team, however, is how it responds to adversity. Obviously, this is not a shocking statement. But it is simple reality. How a team is able to respond to negative experiences is what generally separates a championship team from the rest of the pack.

As coaches, our responsibility is to stay as consistent as possible throughout the season — whether we are winning or losing. Our objective must always be to generate daily improvement from our team regardless of the results of recent games.

External stakeholders will sway greatly throughout a season. Fans and members of the media will tend to be too optimistic about positive things or too negative about areas of concern. We must be a compass for our players and keep them headed in the right direction no matter what the landscape looks like.

After a big win, we must continue to challenge our players to improve in the areas they most need improvement and not allow them to become complacent.

Conversely, after a difficult loss we must identify areas of success we experienced during the loss and build on these successes. It is obvious that building upon a win is much easier than building upon successes inherent in a loss. We are in the confidence-building business and many of our young men are greatly impacted by a loss.

It is incumbent upon us as coaches to keep our players on a steady course throughout the season — even after difficult setbacks. The only way this is possible is for us to be a steadying influence for them at all times.

The moment we as leaders show signs of panic or fear, our team can then question our entire philosophy. If this occurs, the trust we have built amongst the members of our team is now in jeopardy.

However, if we remain strong and steadfast about the direction we are taking the team, chances are they will continue to follow us even during the difficult times. And, if everyone remains together and works to improve everyday, the tough times will soon dissipate.

Arguably the most pivotal game of

our tenure at UNLV was a 14-point loss at nationally ranked Arizona in late November during our third season with the program. While the loss dropped us to 4–2 on the year and had people in Las Vegas publicly questioning the direction of the program, we looked at the loss from a different perspective in our locker room.

We actually led the game for the majority of the first half, and after taking a big punch from the talented Wildcats team, held our own for the final 10 minutes of the game.

Instead of simply accepting the loss as a double-digit defeat to one of the best programs in the nation, we focused on the successful experiences we had. We had gone on the road and hung with arguably the most talented team we would face all year for a large portion of the game.

While a majority of the people removed from the team saw the game as a negative, we decided to view the game as a positive and build upon it. We reinforced the reality to our players that our plan was working and we were improving rather than panicking and reacting to the negative feedback the game generated.

Our team believed the message and worked together to get through the adversity. Almost two months to the day after the Arizona loss, UNLV would crack the Top 25 for the first time in 15 years after winning 15 of our next 17 games, including 10 in a row immediately following the Arizona loss. UNLV was back on the national stage.

The only change after the loss was that our confidence actually improved. Our message was consistent with what we had been preaching for the months leading up to the game, and by sticking to that message after the loss, our players continued to operate in a comfortable atmosphere rather than one of panic and fear.

They trusted us as their coaches and, in return, they rewarded us with amazing team play over the next four months and into the NCAA Tournament.

Post-game

Do your followers know what to expect from you? Or, do they walk around on pins and needles wondering what type of mood the boss is going to be in today?

People perform better in a comfortable yet challenging environment. Comfort is attained through consistent surroundings and your demeanor — as a leader — is an important part of this environment.

The true character of a man can be witnessed during the toughest of times. It's easy to show strong character when things are going well, but the measure of a leader is best taken when there are challenges. During good periods and bad periods, leaders must remain consistent to be trusted.

There is brilliance in consistency. Be brilliant.

Creating an Environment

Pre-game

Too many times we allow the results of our performance dictate the environment in which we operate. In reality, strong leaders emphasize the importance of the environment in which they operate dictate the actual results produced.

People perform better in situations where they want to be. As coaches, we want to put our players in situations they want to be in to allow them to better maximize their potential. Thus, it all starts with practice.

Game Time

Our team's success during a season is a direct result of our performance in workouts from the middle of September through March. While we may play close to 35 games in a season, we may actually practice as a team (including walk-throughs on game days) nearly 150 times during that same season.

As coaches, we are responsible for creating an atmosphere at practice that our players enjoy. Our players should look forward to coming to practice. It should be a place they want to be.

Creating this type of an environment for practice is crucial for several reasons. Primarily, it ensures enhanced dedication from members of the team. Players will come early and stay late if they are in an environment they enjoy. This additional time allows for us not only to improve as a team, but for our players to improve individually. It also helps to avoid the potential distractions of disciplining players for being late or even for missing a practice.

A lively and upbeat practice environment also leads to a better environment for learning and teaching. After all, this is what practice is about. When players are more upbeat they are more receptive to learning. We focus on positive reinforcement throughout most of our practices. However, we do offer constructive criticism when necessary. Our expectations are consistent and very high so, obviously, there is need to offer criticism.

The breakdown of our feedback during practice is close to the 80/20 Rule — 80 percent positive reinforcement, and 20 percent constructive criticism. There are times when making 80 percent of our words positive can be a challenge, but it is important to remain consistent with our players as well as protect the positive practice environment we strive so hard to create.

A key element to creating this desired environment is to set high expectations for each practice session and, as important, to be consistent with those expectations. We expect a lot from our players during our practices on a daily basis, and it is unfair to all of us if those expectations vary. Players need to know what to expect each and every day from our coaching staff.

This is done through appropriately communicating our goals to the players consistently during each practice session. They need to clearly understand the objective of each drill and what we need to do to accomplish the objective. Then, as we work through the drill, we need to provide the proper feedback — again, working with the 80/20 Rule — that helps them achieve the results we want.

Finally, it is imperative we are being as

efficient with our players' time as possible. The number one way to damage an environment is to have someone believe your actions are a waste of his time.

We have an efficient plan for each and every practice. We limit "the standing around" to a minimum, something we know our players appreciate, and also we stay away from the long, drawn-out speeches. Our practices are action-oriented for our players and this helps to protect the lively, upbeat mood we are seeking as well as enhances our conditioning.

To be as efficient as possible we even limit our team film sessions, working to have them last no longer than 10–15 minutes. We want to get in, accomplish what needs to be accomplished, and get out.

In a larger group, it is much more difficult to capture and retain the attention of everyone. We spend longer periods of time working with players one-on-one, both on the court and in the film room. However, when it comes to the overall team practice environment, we don't want to risk losing our efficiency.

Our practices are demanding. However, we never lose sight that our players must look forward to coming to these practices everyday. They are basketball players and they must continue to enjoy playing the game they love.

And the more they enjoy it, the more dedicated and the more receptive to learning they will be.

Post-game

Your overall focus as a leader is to impact results. **Thus, your immediate focus should be to create and maintain a positive working environment for your team.**

A business can only maximize its potential if all of its team members are performing at optimum levels. This occurs when the daily environment for all of the team members is a positive one.

Leaders cannot control every detail inside their respective organizations, nor should they try. However, what we do have control over is the environment in which our team members work on a daily basis.

Simple question: Do your team members look forward to coming to your place of business? Chances are if the answer is no then they are not performing at their maximum potential, and neither is your team.

There are four elements to keep in mind when developing a positive environment:

1. **Be upbeat** — People want to be around people who make them feel good. They are also more receptive to learning in a lively, upbeat environment.

2. **Be consistent** — People want to know what is expected of them everyday. Set high expectations — that is fine as long as you are consistent with them.

3. **Be a communicator** — Provide constant feedback working to achieve 80 percent positive reinforcement balanced with 20 percent constructive criticism. Inform your team of goals and how to best accomplish them.

4. **Be efficient** — Don't be perceived as someone who does not value the time of your team members. Get in and get out.

You will find success in your results if you spend time creating the proper environment.

Positive Praise

Pre-game

Leaders set the tone for nearly every experience their teams encounter. And after the fact, leaders also determine what their teams will take away from that experience.

This responsibility is what ultimately **puts leaders in a position to either encourage their teams to make progress, or cause division and an increased loss of confidence.**

Game Time

Any one practice can be positioned as a positive session or a negative session depending on how we, the coaches, choose to look at it.

This is powerful, yet it can also be dangerous.

If we consistently choose to dwell only on the skills the players did not do as well as we expected, practice then becomes a negative in the eyes of the players.

Instead, we choose on a daily basis to emphasize the positive more, helping to build our players' confidence levels. That is not to say there are not times in a season when we need to challenge our players aggressively and hold them accountable for the things they are not doing correctly. However, we make sure doing this through negative feedback does not become the norm.

Instead, we are convinced players react better to feedback in the form of positive praise.

In fact, we believe 80 percent of what we tell the players should be positive and only 20 percent — at the most — should be criticism, or something a player might classify as negative.

For example, if we are working with a big man on being more aggressive on the boards, we will want to focus a comment on a particular instance where he delivered for the team with an important rebound in a recent game.

Walking around before practice the day after a game I may say something like: "Andrew, you did a great job fighting for that rebound last night with a minute to go when we were up by five. They could have made it a three-point game, but your rebound helped us stretch it to seven and sealed the win. That's what we need from you. Great job. Keep it up."

While the fact may be the player did not deliver in other instances during the same game, the positive praise reinforces what we are expecting from the player.

Later, when the team is watching film together, we will make sure to publicly point out the same thing and give even more positive praise.

"That's what we need from you right there, Andrew," I may say in front of the entire team. "That rebound was huge. It helped us seal the game. If you keep doing things like that, you can help us go a long way."

During a practice, we will also take notice of the things we need players to work on. If the same player were to gather in a rebound during a drill, we might shout out. "That's it, Andrew. That's what we need."

The player is much more apt to be responsive to receiving this positive praise than he is to be getting chewed out each and every time he does not haul in a rebound.

In fact, he begins to seek the positive feedback. When he is not delivering, he is not receiving the positive input he is now seeking. This motivates him to raise his performance. The unsaid can often be as powerful as the said — but not as harmful to a person's confidence.

In this type of situation, a "negative" comment that may be used is: "Come on, Andrew. That's the type of board we need you to come away with. You can get that board! Let's pull that one in next time."

The negative comment is designed in a way that does not ridicule the player. Instead, it is positioned in a way that puts him at the same level of understanding as the coach. Yes, the player knows he needs to get to that rebound. And, in fact, because he did not, it hurt the team — notice the use of the term "we." Also, the use of the term "let's" puts us together trying to get this task accomplished.

Delivering positive praise should become second nature to our coaches. However, there are times during a season where we are challenged to stay positive. Usually these are the times we need to be more positive than ever. **Coaches must remember we offer security for our players.** When we are playing on the road in front of 15,000 hostile fans, we may have a player make a poor decision, which leads to a negative result. No matter how badly this may frustrate us at that moment, the reality is there is a young man on our team who just made a mistake in front of 15,000 other people and he is desperately looking for someone to be on his side. That someone has to be you — because there is no one else.

A coach is in a very powerful position with the psyches of his players. You can choose to make almost any experience a positive or a negative one. Choosing positive a large majority of the time will deliver more results over the long run.

Post-game

Think about your team members. Who is on their side everyday? Clients? Potential clients? Vendors? Chances are your team members battle everyday through negative or potentially negative situations with people in environments that you cannot control.

But as the leader, you do control your environment and your team members need you to develop a positive place for them to come to day-in and day-out. You offer them the security they need to deliver the results you want.

People are motivated by positive praise. The strongest leaders of teams are masters at utilizing this method of feedback.

Positive praise helps to build a strong environment as well as helps to raise the confidence levels of those on your team. This is not to say that team members in a positive praise environment are not held responsible for their actions.

In fact, the trust you build through leading a positive praise environment will allow you to demand even more from your team members than if the environment was a constant negative setting.

Because positive praise leaders build more trust they increase the loyalty levels their team members feel for them. This loyalty leads to increased personal ownership in the process from team members and enhanced results.

Being an effective leader is not about demanding respect. It's about communicating in a positive way that builds respect for you.

The Failure Cycle

Pre-game

Failure is not an action. It is a consequence of previous actions or a previous lack of actions. Unfortunately, **failure begets additional failure, which ultimately fuels the failure cycle**.

Leaders must continuously teach their followers the value of habits that avoid the cyclical nature of failure. This calls for us to educate our followers on how to pro-actively anticipate the consequences of actions prior to those consequences becoming a reality.

Teaching our followers that failure is a cycle is not enough. We must teach our followers the habits that will help them avoid getting caught in the failure cycle.

Game Time

Almost every collegiate coach who has been in his or her profession any amount of time has dealt with a student-athlete struggling academically. This is bound to happen in college with athletes and non-athletes alike.

When this situation occurs, more often than not the genesis of the problem begins with personal habits of the individual struggling in school — habits that often create poor decisions.

This leads the player into **step one of the failure cycle — falling behind by not taking care of the basics**.

The player typically falls behind initially in a class because he doesn't do something basic like read the daily assignment or he misses a lecture. This may occur because of the student making a choice to attend a social function rather than reading one night or staying out too late and not making it to class in the morning.

If these choices become routine, which they often do, it leads to more missed assignments or missed lectures. Now the player is headed towards **step two in the failure cycle — cutting corners**.

113

In this step, the player now faces an exam in the class where he has failed to do the basics such as staying up on his work on a daily basis. Instead of studying properly for the exam and reviewing the information he should have already learned, he is now forced to try to cut corners by cramming prior to the test in an effort to learn everything he needs to know.

Cutting corners leaves him wide open for *step three* **of the failure cycle — making mistakes**. The player then proceeds to not perform to his ability on the exam, which leads to the mistake — a poor grade.

Obviously, the mistake is usually the most tangible element of the failure cycle. And, for some, the mistake is misunderstood as the improper action. However, the mistake is actually the outcome of the prior negative actions. Now that the actions are measurable, failure becomes tangible.

But the cycle does not end here because of *step four* — **the consequences**. There are consequences for the mistake. In the example using the player, he may now face an increased workload to make up for the bad grade. Academically, this will increase the pressure on him for that particular class, which may impact him in other classes.

This is where the cycle begins to repeat itself by returning to step one — falling behind by not taking care of the basics.

Because of the initial failure, the player's basic responsibilities are now increased and the chances of him falling behind again are actually greater. He will have to spend so much time trying to make up for his mistake that he will soon have to start cutting corners in other areas, leaving himself open for new mistakes.

The cycle also picks up intensity as the failure may be transferred to other parts of his life. There is a chance his playing status can be impacted due to the failure in the class. If he is not eligible to play, he may begin a new failure cycle when it comes to his performance on the court. Without playing time, he is not doing the basic things he needs to do to improve himself as a player and a new cycle is set in motion.

What started as a few small and seemingly insignificant decisions have now become life-altering for the player. That is the danger of the failure cycle.

Post-game

The danger of teaching the failure cycle is its simplicity. People have to value good habits to value the cycle and the truth it reveals.

Strong leaders are effective at preventing the first two steps of the failure cycle so that step three — the mistake — seldom occurs. Poor leaders find themselves focusing primarily on step four — the consequences — after the mistake is made, which ultimately leads their teams back into step one of the cycle. This, of course, is how teams are led into failure.

Two of the most common weaknesses found in organizations every day are poor organizational and communication skills. These two traits lead to the majority of failure cycles in our world.

Good organizations led by strong leaders focus a great deal of time and energy on improving their team members' personal organizational and communication skills. Not only do leaders teach their team members how to do it, they also teach them the value of the improved habits and how to avoid the failure cycle.

Leaders should not be experts at helping people through the failure cycle. **They should be experts at helping people to *avoid* the failure cycle.**

It's amazing to think how simple, yet productive, life can be if we only take care of the basic expectations each day.

The Success Cycle

Pre-game

People are not successful by accident. As it has been said many times before, it is by design.

Just as failure has its own cycle, the success cycle also exists.

Success starts with taking care of one's basic responsibilities on a daily basis. The rest becomes habitual.

Game Time

The entire philosophy of our program is based on helping our players develop habits that will improve them as both basketball players and students and, ultimately, as young men. We want our players to leave our system prepared for life — whether they play basketball professionally or not.

When every player first arrives on campus to become a part of our program, we ask him his expectations for his time with us. Through this process we help each player put together an individual success plan of which he takes ownership. The player not only outlines what he hopes to accomplish, he also outlines what he has to do to make this a reality.

This tangible plan is crucial for the long-term development of the student-athlete. The goals and objectives serve as a constant reminder to him about where he is headed. We meet with our players weekly to review these plans and provide feedback. Are we getting results? If so, why? Are we not getting results? If not, why?

We try to focus as much as possible on positive praise to help our guys through their college experience. That praise, however, does not focus on just hitting major benchmarks. In fact, most of the praise (when it comes to helping our players through their personal success plans) is regarding their daily decisions. After all, this is where the success cycle begins.

Success is obtained when a person possesses the habits that allow him to continually make correct decisions. It is all part of the success cycle. The steps of the success cycle mirror those of the failure cycle.

Step one — **do the basic things you need to do everyday.** We preach non-stop to our players about doing what they need to do at the time they need to do it. This is obtainable by having strong time management and organizational skills, which allows them to identify priorities correctly.

If the basics are covered on a daily basis, then they enter *step two* **of the success cycle — no short cuts.** Not having to take short cuts greatly reduces the risk of mistakes. In fact, it allows for enough time to correct mistakes if needed, and this leads to a successful experience.

This is *step three* **of the success cycle — experiencing the victory.** Once again, this is the most tangible element of the cycle. However, our objective is to work with our players to help them understand why they succeeded. We constantly give them positive praise for what they did in step one rather than simply praising them on the success.

Finally, *step four* **of the success cycle — the consequences** — occurs. In this step, a person gains confidence and may even gain accolades for his victory. This is another form of positive praise that reassures the person what he is doing is correct, and leads him to start the cycle over again at step one.

This cycle not only works for individuals, it also works for teams.

College basketball teams that are awarded championships in March and April actually begin winning them in August, September and October of the previous year. They do this by developing productive habits in preseason conditioning and training camp. This allows them to master the basics, which means they will not be trying to catch up later in the season when all of the chips are on the table.

A day that we do not improve as a team in October is a day that will cost us come tournament time. One of our biggest challenges as coaches is to instill this philosophy in our young players and help them see that *step one* of the success cycle is the most important step.

Post-game

People don't make a habit out of being successful. They are successful because of their habits.

However, so much emphasis is put on the actual victories and the success itself that it is easy for us to overlook the decisions made that ultimately lead to the moment of success.

As a leader, you are responsible for leading your team into its own success cycle as well as leading your team members into their own personal success cycles. The most productive way to do this is to continuously emphasize the correct decisions that are being made on a daily basis that lead to bigger moments of success.

Map out individual success plans with members of your team and have them tell you what it will take on a daily basis for them to follow those plans and obtain the goals and objectives that they identified. Continually measure the progress made — or not made — focusing on the results of daily actions and habits.

Share the success cycle with your team and provide them as much sincere positive praise as possible, which continually reinforces the importance of taking care of the basics on a daily basis.

If they do this, the force of the cycle will inevitably lead them to the special moment of enjoying the positive consequences of victory.

Controlled Spontaneity

Pre-game

Our lives are made up of millions of split-second decisions. Obviously, we cannot prepare for each and every individual decision.

However, we can prepare ourselves to consistently make decisions that are in the best interest of our overall wellbeing. As leaders, we must teach others to value this form of decision-making as well.

We must seek to find control of ourselves, and others, in this spontaneous world.

Game Time

Basketball is a game of continuous action. With each action brings the need for spontaneous adjustments.

While these adjustments are usually split-second decisions made by individual players in the heat of battle, it is our responsibility as coaches to prepare our players for those moments.

There are so many variables that go into the different actions that might occur on the court. How is the opponent going to react? How are teammates going to react? How much time is left in the game? What is the score?

Because of this, we must teach our players conceptually rather than robotically. Our objective is to have our players grasp the concept for what we want to accomplish — not simply tell them what to do. If they understand the concept of the objective and value it, they will have a much better chance of actually achieving the objective.

For instance, when we call a play, we cannot predict 100 percent of the time what an opponent is going to do. But by having our players not only understand how to run the play, but also the reasoning behind the play, we have a better chance of success.

We may tell our players, "If we run this play, this opponent is going to do one of three things and here are the three things: A, B and C." We don't know exactly what he is going to do, but by our players understanding the intent of the play, they are better prepared to react to any situation, because they have now been elevated to the level of decision-maker, not simply direction-follower.

As coaches, we can't control every decision our players make on the floor. However, we must develop an environment that aligns our players' split-second decisions with our preferences. This is done by teaching our players conceptually as well as providing constant feedback and — when possible — positive praise about correct decisions.

This also applies off the court. We consistently talk to our players about the consequences of their decisions away from basketball. In fact, at the end of practice every Friday, we talk about decision-making and discuss different situations they may encounter over the weekend.

A major philosophy we share with our players is that **good decisions are expected — not applauded**. In life, we may make 100 good decisions, but if we make one poor decision, that decision may have a far greater impact on us than any of the good ones.

We work with our players to visualize themselves in possible negative situations. "You are at a gathering and a fight is brewing," is a topic we might discuss. It is important that our players have thoroughly thought through all of the options that they have at a moment like this. Unfortunately, most people do not take the initiative to weigh the consequences of something like this happening prior to actually being caught up in the moment. Once the consequences are reviewed, it is easy to see the option of removing yourself from the situation is almost always the best choice.

By educating our players about the concept of walking away — and not just telling them to walk away — they are more inclined to see the big picture and understand the objective of the tactic.

Does this type of training guarantee players will always make the decisions you want them to make on and off the court? Of course not. However, it is the best way possible for us to try to positively control the spontaneity of the games and, most importantly, the lives of the young men in our program.

Post-game

A team is an extension of its leader. Thus, the leader is responsible for aligning his team members' decision-making processes with his.

Poor leaders will dictate to members of their teams what they are supposed to do and expect people to follow simply because the leader said so. Those same leaders will then be frustrated when the same bad decisions are made over and over.

Conversely, strong leaders are committed to educating their team members about concepts, not solely individual situations. They walk teammates through the decision-making process and provide information about possible variables that might arise and how those might impact the objective. Strong leaders will follow-up with continual feedback and positive praise.

This process allows team members to be better aligned with the wants of the leader as well as possess a better understanding of the overall impact their decisions have on the wellbeing of the team.

Our team members make hundreds, even thousands, of split-second decisions on a daily basis without our direct consultation. The culmination of the results of these decisions ultimately decides our effectiveness as teams and as leaders. And, like with individuals, one bad decision can outweigh 100 good ones.

A leader is only as strong as his team. **Make the investment to develop a team of great decision-makers and you will become a great leader.**

Leave Them Feeling Special

Pre-game

The most valuable possessions we have in our lives are our relationships. Nothing is worth more.

During the recruiting process, we emphasize the significance of quality relationships — player/player and player/coaching staff — more than anything else.

Relationships are shaped through the many conversations we have with people throughout our days — both formal and informal. Although these relationships actually define us as individuals, we seldom put very much thought into most of our interactions with other people.

Sure we might think about what we want to say in the big meeting or to the potential client or recruit that could help us. But what amount of time do we put into thinking about what to say to a waitress or the stranger we are standing with in a line?

These moments, of course, are more difficult to prepare for individually. **What if we had an objective for each and every encounter we have with someone throughout the day — to leave them feeling special?**

Too often, we decide how to treat others based on what they can do for us. This is an attitude that results in shallow relations and efforts that lack sincerity.

Whether we know a person or not or whether we perceive that they can help us or not — it should not matter. It should be our objective to leave them feeling special, leave them feeling good about themselves.

Imagine what an amazing world we would live in if everyone tried to live by this one simple rule.

Game Time

Our daughter, Angie, has a true gift. She is blessed with not only understanding how to make other people feel special, but she is very aware that she has been given this gift and chooses to use it simply to make others feel good about themselves.

In fact, I believe this is her best trait. And that is saying a lot as she has many good ones. (I guess she took more after her mother than she did me.)

Angie has an objective that anytime she speaks to anyone she wants to leave that person feeling good about himself or herself. She consistently goes out of her way to accomplish this.

Because of this trait, people of all ages and backgrounds are attracted to her. They want to be around her and, many times, they may not understand why. She radiates joy by making everyone else the center of attention in a positive light. I have been around a lot of skilled communicators in my life, but I have never met any more skilled than Angie in this area.

The reason she is so successful at this is because her motives are sincere — she truly wants other people to feel good about themselves. She is less than a year away from finishing her residency as an OB/GYN and I can't think of a better profession for her to use this skill. She makes expectant mothers feel like the center of the world and that is exactly how they deserve to feel.

Although Angie came by some of this naturally, **it's important to recognize that she has made a choice to work to make people feel good about themselves and that is a choice we can all make**.

I believe you can tell a lot about someone by the way they treat the wait staff at restaurants or the support staff in other venues. Because of the position Barb and I have been in over the past 25 years, a lot of people automatically treat us with respect and go out of their way to try and make us feel special. However, I am very interested in seeing how those same people treat other people who are not in the public eye like we are. This is where sincerity comes in and I appreciate those who treat all people with respect.

When it comes to relationships, status should be irrelevant in regards to kindness.

We try very hard to educate our players about the positions we hold in our community as members of a basketball team. People are initially attracted to us because of the position — not because who we are as individuals. Our goal should be to impress them as individuals and use our position as a platform for doing good things.

It all begins with making individuals feel special about themselves every time we are with them. And the reality is this is something that is very easy to do. It can be as simple as a sincere smile or thank you. It can be as simple as remembering someone by name or asking someone how things are going in their life — and actually taking the time to listen.

Making someone feel special does not take much effort at all. And that's the sad part. Even though it is so easy, few take the initiative to actually do it. But you can tell the people who do. People like Angie, they brighten up your day.

Post-game

This may be the simplest way to set yourself apart in the eyes of others.

Gifted leaders have the unique skill of making people feel good about themselves. These leaders have made a conscious decision to lift other people up constantly.

Whether you are speaking with the CEO of a company you are hoping to do work for or simply exchanging pleasantries with support staff in any setting, you have the opportunity to make someone feel good about themselves.

And the more visible your position is, the

more of an impact you can have. This is particularly important in your place of work. Many times we take for granted the people closest to us and treat them more poorly than other people. We must not allow ourselves to fall into the habit of giving the people closest to us — our team members, family members, etc. — the "remains of our day." Because we have a comfort level with these people, we need to be very conscious about our efforts to make them feel special.

Our days may be tough and exhausting, but as leaders, you cannot give the people closest to you simply what is remaining of your day. They deserve more.

Be in the Moment

Pre-game

People deserve to have our undivided attention when we are with them. This goes for teammates to family members to people servicing us in stores and restaurants.

It's easy to get lost in the cares of our own world and not be fully engaged when dealing with others. However, we must make a conscious decision to be in the moment with the person or people we are currently in contact with. **Not only will people appreciate us for being more engaged, we will also be able to better retain information that**

can be beneficial for our relationships in the future.

It costs nothing to give someone your undivided attention. But the returns may be priceless.

Game Time

Not everyone is naturally a good listener. But there is one simple way we can all work on becoming one — learn to ask questions.

Asking questions not only encourages people to feel free to talk, it also requires us to become active listeners. It's amazing how much we can learn by simply asking someone a question and truly listening to the answer.

Our objective should be to talk to people or listen to people in a way that makes them feel good about themselves. There is one easy way to accomplish this — talk to someone else about himself or herself. People love talking about themselves — their families, their jobs, their interests, their experiences. This isn't a bad thing; it's just a natural thing. People are comfortable talking about what they know and if you ask them questions about these things, you will put them at ease and they will find you more enjoyable to be around.

Because of the nature of our positions,

Barb and I find ourselves on many occasions spending time with people with whom we are just getting acquainted. I'm sure there have been many people we were meeting for the first time over a lunch or dinner that thought they would be spending an hour talking about basketball, our careers and our team. Barb and I, however, would rather find out more about them and their interests.

We have developed so many good friends throughout the years by simply asking questions when we first meet people. And, as importantly, we make an effort to retain as much information as possible to connect with the people when we see them the next time. Nothing makes us — as people — feel better than when another person recalls something of interest to us and addresses it.

The obvious place to start with recalling information is by remembering the names of people. There is nothing more personal to someone else than his or her own name. It is so simple, yet true. And, unfortunately, this is a fact that many of us tend to overlook. When we first meet people, our mind is trying to figure out the person's position and maybe even how he or she can help us — if, in fact, they can. Instead, we should remain in the moment and try to brand his or her name into our memory.

As a younger man, like many people, I struggled with remembering names. During my college years, however, I began to make a concerted effort in this area. This is the first step in working to become better with names — consciously deciding to make an effort. Ultimately, this is what people deserve.

There are a few tricks that go along the way. Free feel to ask people to repeat their names when you first meet them or use it back immediately to confirm that you heard the name right. Then, and this one really makes people feel special, use their name in your conversation soon after meeting them.

To me it has become a game in which I challenge myself. That is especially true when it comes to the basketball camps that we put on for youngsters every summer. Our camps typically open on a Sunday afternoon and end on the following Wednesday. As a younger coach, it was my goal to know the names of all of the campers — sometimes as many as 300 of them — by Tuesday morning. There is nothing better than speaking with a parent and identifying his or her child by name in front of them. It just makes everyone feel special.

There are other practices we have tried to employ as well to help with being in the moment with the people we are around.

Because of Dad's passion for baseball, we grew up loving the car radio. As a child in Kansas, I would spend hours upon hours sitting alone in the parked car outside of our house listening to baseball games because the car radio picked up the stations much clearer than any radios inside of the house.

However, the car radio has since become a thing of the past for me in an effort to become a more engaged listener.

I'm not sure if Angie and Kevin — our kids — enjoyed it when it was happening, but it was special to me as a father. **Every morning I made a point not to have the radio on during our trips to school.** It seemed like it would be too easy to have the radio on — it would simply be an excuse not to talk. I would be listening to either sports or news or the kids listening to their music.

I am sure there are some days the kids wish that we had the radio on instead of having to talk with their dad. And, I know there are some days we drove to school with more silence than conversation.

But overall, the experience gave me time to truly talk with my kids on a daily basis. I made an effort to give them my undivided attention and in return I received something most of us parents struggle to ever get — our kids' undivided attention.

Angie and Kevin are tremendous people. Barb and I adore the relationship we share with both of them as their parents and they continue to amaze us as we watch them grow into fine young individuals.

As I examine how my relationship with my

children grew over time, I believe the simple decision to turn the car radio off and fully engage my kids every morning while driving them to school helped to lay the foundation.

Another way to practice a form of being in the moment is with the use of our cell phones.

Too often we are tempted to answer our phones while already engaged in conversations with other people. Are we saying the person on the phone is more important than the person right in front of us?

Family responsibilities and emergencies are legit, however, a vast majority of our calls can easily be pushed to voicemail out of respect for the people who are already giving us their moment.

If it sounds simple, that's because it is. Game planning is always the easy part. It's the execution of the plan that determines the outcome.

Post-game

Some leaders might believe they are too busy to worry about the small things. Unfortunately, the small things always involve people and the last thing people want to feel is small or insignificant.

Effective leaders have an ability to make other people feel good about themselves and to make people understand they are significant. And, in any type of organization, everyone plays a specific role and the best organizations are the ones getting the most out of all of their players in every role.

One of your top priorities as a leader should be to engage with your team members — or anyone, for that matter — to make them feel significant. Let them know they matter to you.

When you talk with them be in the moment and pick up on small details — is someone in their family not healthy, are they struggling with a client, is something special going on with one of her children? At a later time, follow-up on the personal situation and be a sincere listener. Nothing will make people feel more important.

The more important you make people feel about themselves the more important you become in their eyes. And the more important you become in their eyes the more they are willing to deliver for you, their leader.

If You Don't Have Anything Nice to Say

Pre-game

Clichés are interesting.

The reality is they express a popular — and usually important — idea. However, because of overuse, they can lose their impact on people. People stop listening to the message as soon as they hear the words. It's an automatic function of the human brain.

Now imagine hearing a cliché for the first time and truly contemplating its meaning. It can be powerful.

But even more powerful — try living the meaning.

That's what Dad wanted us to do with one

of his favorite lessons: **"If you don't have anything nice to say, don't say anything at all."**

For us Kruger kids, that was not a cliché. That was a way of life — and Dad made sure of it.

If everyone lived by this simple rule, how great would it be to live in that world?

Game Time

I like working with members of the media and I have a great amount of respect for what they do.

If it wasn't for the interest from the media, which represents the general public's interest, we would not be blessed to enjoy the lifestyle that we have.

That being said, I'm sure I drive some members of the press a little insane. Why? Because they view me as boring. As just a good ol' boy from Silver Lake, Kansas, shooting out nothing but vanilla quote after vanilla quote making their job a little more difficult.

Sample quote from the middle of our 2006–07 Sweet 16 season at UNLV: "Obviously, we need to get better. We have to keep working hard everyday in practice to improve as a team. We're playing solidly on defense most of the time, however, we have to be aggressive and get after it the entire 40 minutes."

OK, I will admit most readers probably begin to gloss over these types of statements in the morning paper after a while.

But there are two things to point out:

1. When I say things like that, I truly believe it. This is not rocket science (cliché alert), which is why I find myself tending to lead with something like "obviously." If you improve everyday in practice and play tough defense, you will win ballgames and a lot of them. Our 2006–07 UNLV team — picked to finish sixth in the conference — followed this recipe and was within two baskets of advancing to the Elite Eight.

2. My responsibility is to protect our players, their families and the university we represent while winning basketball games in the process. Being aware of this makes me very cautious of what I say in interviews and keeps away the damage caused by gossip.

I enjoy colorful quotes and soundbites as much as the next guy. However, Dad taught us an important thing about humor — **it usually comes at someone else's expense**.

Some coaches use the press to get a message across to individual players. Other coaches try to entertain at the expense of members of the press or even their teams.

Everyone has their own style with which they are the most comfortable. But what we have found is we must remember our players are big fans of college basketball and big fans of our own programs. These are young, impressionable people who read the papers, listen to the radio and visit websites.

Unfortunately, there is no accountability for what is said by some in chat rooms, letters to the editor or on radio call-in shows. Our players deal with enough negativity from these sometimes irresponsible "fans" to also have to worry about coaches calling them out in the media or taking a shot at them — even from a distance.

We get after our players behind closed doors. If they are not meeting expectations, we let them know about it.

However, when it comes to the media, I will gladly take the public wrath of a journalist who is frustrated with my blandness before ever coming close to insulting or embarrassing one of our players through a media outlet. It is important that our players have confidence in us to handle things in this way.

It's a simple guideline. We want to treat our players as I would want my own son to be treated.

That's just the way Dad taught us to do it.

Post-game

As a leader in an organization, you may not find yourself interviewed by beat writers, but you still must act as if you will be held accountable for everything you say.

The informal channels of communications within organizations are many times much more powerful than the formal channels of communications.

The basis for strong leadership is trust, and you build trust by treating people fairly. **Nothing is more disruptive to this leadership cycle than your fairness being questioned.**

Speaking negatively about people in front of others or being humorous at the expense of others can be damaging for several reasons. First, if that person is present or word gets back to him, your fairness is severely jeopardized. Second, others notice how you ridicule someone else in front of others and they begin to fear what you might do to them at some point or what you are doing to them already behind their backs.

There is a time and place to give negative feedback to someone. It should be with that person and as few others as possible. If that is not effective then the next step is to call on peer pressure. However, it rarely gets to this point, especially if the individual is genuine in his desire to achieve.

If you want to add in humor, try using targets that aren't as personal or offensive. You must be more creative this way, but a good place to start is with yourself. Many secure leaders are known for their self-deprecating humor because, while entertaining others, it also shows confidence and builds trust. (Note: If you aren't comfortable using yourself as a target for your own humor, imagine what other people feel like when you use them.)

As a leader in any type of organization, you must always be aware of what you are saying and how it can be construed, whether you are in a professional or private setting. It's not what you say, but what others hear that really matters. We always emphasize to our players that when they are being quoted they must visualize how their comments will read to the public eye.

Leaders must do the same thing. The cameras and tape recorders may not be rolling, but whatever you say is always "on the record."

Not What You Say, But What They Hear

Pre-game

The ability to communicate is powerful.

Without communication, great ideas or institutional knowledge are limited in their usefulness.

However, communication has as much to do with the people hearing the message as its does with the person trying to communicate the message.

Don't ever underestimate your audience and what it hears you saying.

Game Time

There were less than 10 seconds remaining in the game.

We were trailing by a basket and had the ball out of bounds on the sideline. We called a timeout.

The band was playing, the fans were screaming and the cheerleaders were on the court.

As usual, everyone huddled around me in the timeout. I had my board and drew up the out-of-bounds play that would hopefully tie up the game. We quickly addressed what all five guys would be doing and we broke the huddle.

I was confident we would get a good look at the basket. We would have a solid opportunity to score if we were able to implement what we drew up in the timeout.

But there was one problem. The guy I wanted to receive the in-bounds pass and control the flow of the play was the guy getting ready to pass the ball in-bounds.

"Time out!" I yelled. And, literally, we went back to the drawing board.

I cannot recall what eventually happened in that particular game, but to this day I remember the life lesson I learned from that night: "It is not about what you say. It is about what people hear."

As the head coach, I ultimately have to take

responsibility for that situation. Even though I may have described perfectly — in my mind — what I wanted the players to do, there was an obvious breakdown between what I said and what they heard.

And, because they were the ones implementing the plan, the only relevant part of the equation is "what they heard."

This is true when communicating with any audience at any time — not just in the heat of the moment. Understanding your audience is the most critical part of communicating.

As a basketball team, one of the most inefficient uses of our time is to re-teach something in practice. We must use our practice time to improve and enhance, not completely re-teach. Our responsibility as coaches is to make sure our team members fully understand what it is we are trying to communicate to them when we initially teach a specific drill or tactic.

If we show up at a later practice and the guys are not 100 percent clear on what was taught to them initially, that responsibility falls directly on our coaching staff — not the players.

This is a mindset our coaching staff must have. It puts the initial burden on the people — the coaches — who are trying to transfer the knowledge. This makes us pay better attention to the way we are communicating with our players.

We may know what it is that we are trying to say, but if our players have not received that message we have failed at communicating. And if we fail at communicating to our team, we fail as coaches.

Post-game

When your team members listen to what you are saying, do they hear what you are saying? By taking responsibility for what they hear, you are more likely to better communicate with your team.

"Hearing" involves meaning and emotion. This takes personal biases and past experiences of the individual listener and combines them with your spoken words to create a perceived message.

One way to help increase the effectiveness of your communication with team members is to ask them for clarification. "Are you good with that?" "Do you have any concerns?" "Is there anything I can do to help you with that?"

Another method is to clarify the message for yourself with them. "Just so I am on the right track, I am going to do _____ and you are going to do _____."

These are tactics that may help you to better communicate. However, the most important factor in increasing what your team members hear is holding yourself accountable for what they hear from you. This will make you spend the proper amount of time and focus on clearly communicating your thoughts and objectives.

Often times, leaders have so much institutional knowledge that we make the mistake of speaking to others as if they share that same amount of institutional knowledge. This is our fault and no one else's.

Take the time to communicate clearly with your team members. If you take ownership of what they hear, you'll be rewarded by their production.

A Team of Individuals

Pre-game

Coaches may be responsible for an entire team, but a team is made up of individuals. And in sports, as in all aspects of life, not all individuals respond the same to feedback nor are they motivated by the same techniques.

Thus, this is where true leadership must be displayed. How do you treat players separately — to best motivate or critique them as individuals — while still respecting the team as a group? **It's the balance of leading a team of individuals.** And the basis for it all is fairness.

If players fully realize that you have their best interests at heart, then anything is possible.

Game Time

I never get tired of telling the story of Joel Anthony, a senior center on our 2006–07 Sweet 16 team at UNLV.

Joel joined us in our first year in Las Vegas as a junior college transfer. He played sparingly his first season with us before we convinced Joel that by redshirting a year, he would make a big impact his senior year and also have a chance to play this game professionally for many years to come.

At the time not only did most fans chuckle at the notion, even Joel truly didn't believe in his heart that playing beyond college was an option.

Then he went to work. By the time his senior season came around, Joel had turned himself into one of the finest shot blockers I have ever seen. He also worked hard to become a viable option on offense in the low post with his back to the basket.

However, despite a tremendous preseason, five games into the season Joel was struggling with confidence. So we moved him to the bench — knowing he was emotionally strong enough to handle the change — and inserted fellow senior center Gaston Essengue into the starting lineup.

Things clicked. We went on a 10-game winning streak including wins at nationally ranked University of Nevada–Reno and on national television against Texas Tech, with Bobby Knight seeking the all-time wins mark against us.

While Gaston gave us a spark with his mid-range jumper, Joel began to get his confidence back coming off the bench and became a force to be reckoned with on the court, particularly on the defensive end.

Early in league play, Joel was clearly playing better than Gaston and deserved the chance to start again. However, that would have presented a problem for us — what would that do to Gaston's individual confidence? We needed our senior center combo to be clicking for us to compete against good big men and we were worried Gaston's productivity would decrease.

Gaston, as a sensitive individual, would probably not handle the situation as positively from a confidence standpoint as Joel did when he was removed from the starting lineup. After all, Gaston had been playing well for us and we were winning, but he wasn't playing better than Joel.

But we also had to consider the other players. They knew Joel deserved the chance to reclaim his starting role and what type of

153

message did that send if we did not address the situation.

I went to Joel to discuss our concern. And Joel delivered once again.

"No problem, Coach," he said. "Let's do whatever is best for the team."

Joel knew Gaston was a big part of our success and he was one of Gaston's biggest fans. **He knew Gaston had to play well for our team to compete at a high level.** Joel sacrificed individually so the team could achieve maximum results.

So Gaston stayed in the starting lineup, Joel came off the bench, and our senior center combo averaged 12.8 points, 9.1 rebounds and 4.3 blocked shots per game and helped lead us to 30 victories.

In one of those wins, our "backup" center, Joel, keyed a second half rally against TCU with a Mountain West Conference record 13 blocked shots in one of the finest displays of defense I have been around in my entire career.

When it came time for the post-season accolades, it did not matter that Joel came off the bench as he was selected the Mountain West Conference's Defensive Player of the Year as well as UNLV's Male Sportsman of the Year.

And although Joel did not get drafted, by the time draft night was over, he had signed an impressive free agent contract with the NBA's Miami Heat and went on to enjoy his rookie season with the Heat.

Indeed, by helping the team, this young individual was continuing his basketball career after college. Why? Because he trusted that all our decisions were fair and were made with his best interests at heart. And, more importantly, they were.

Post-game

It's easy for leaders to make the assumption that "being fair" means treating everyone the exact same way under the same circumstances. **However, "being fair" is based more on the results you want for people rather than the way you try to help them attain those results.**

Take two sales representatives for example. If they both have realistic individual monthly sales goals set for them and they agree that these goals are realistic and each have a plan of action to try and reach the goals, then it's safe to say at this point — relative to expectations — they are being treated fairly, correct?

What if one of them is driven by the notion of believing it's him against the world? He likes when people tell him "no" or that he won't be able to do things. In fact, where there is not conflict, he creates conflict to keep motivated.

155

Now imagine the other sales representative is more on the sensitive side. He likes to work in a positive environment and continually be told what he is doing well. He is motivated by praise, and the more praise he gets, the more results he delivers.

If you were the leader of a sales team featuring these two types of individuals, would it be fair to treat them the exact same way under the same circumstances? Obviously the answer is no.

It would not be in the best interest of those individuals, your sales team, and, of course, your organization.

Your job as a leader is to understand the individuals that make up your team and work with them as individuals for the betterment of the team.

By being fair to the individuals you are being fair to the team and achieving maximum results.

Make a Play for a Teammate

Pre-game

Successful individuals come from successful teams.

Successful teams are not made up of individuals who are concentrating on individual success and accolades. Instead, these teams are made up of strong individuals who are striving to make their teammates look good.

And in the end, these individuals will receive the due accolades.

Game Time

"Make a play for a teammate."

This is at the heart of our program. Everything that we strive to do as a team surrounds this simple philosophy.

On the court, we want our guys to make plays for teammates. Set a strong pick. Look for the open man. Finish when you get set-up. **Our players should be playing to make their teammates on the court with them look good.** Only when all of our players are doing this at the same time are we most likely to maximize our potential.

This, of course, does not start in games. It starts in practice. We preach to our guys every single day in practice to make a play for a teammate.

As coaches, it is then our responsibility to make sure we are identifying when players are in fact making plays for a teammate and giving consistent positive feedback about the efforts. Eventually, making a play for a teammate should become second nature.

Off the court, nothing changes. We want our players to have the mindset of always making their teammates look good. Performances during press conferences and post-game interviews are tremendous opportunities for this. Our players are encouraged to think about how their responses to questions will read to the readers in tomorrow's newspaper.

If a player is coming off of a big 30-point effort to help lead us to the win, he has a great platform in a post-game interview now to help his teammates look good. Chances are his teammates spent the past 40 minutes helping him to be the star on the court and the least he can do is give them praise in an interview. Even after great individual performances, we encourage our players to talk about teammates over self.

It's been rewarding for us throughout the years to see players mature in their interviews as they take more ownership of the philosophy of making teammates look good. Numerous times I have had reporters approach me and jokingly say they enjoyed a certain player's interviews more as a freshman than as a junior or senior because now the player sounds like me — boring. I will be the first to admit I am not the sound bite machine many coaches are. However, our philosophy is not about flashiness or controversy — it's about making others look good.

This belief of making our teammates look good also leads to non-basketball related issues such as how we perform in the classroom or how we act out at a party on a weekend night. Our players must understand the consequences of their actions and how their actions will impact all of the people associated with our team.

In return, as coaches, we also understand our role is to make plays for our teammates. I strongly believe that if a player fails, it is because I have not put him in the correct position to succeed. It is my responsibility to identify the role in which he will excel and put him in that role. If he fails it is because I have failed. However, if I can correctly identify a role for him that will play to his strengths, I will make a play for him and he will succeed. In return, he is a making a play for me, and helping me to succeed as a coach.

Living by this philosophy day-in and day-out is not always easy. If it were, more teams in all walks of life would enjoy greater amounts of success.

Athletes, by nature, are extremely competitive and prideful. If our players did not take ownership of their personal performances, they would not be playing Division I basketball.

Understanding this, we teach our players that individual accolades come from winning as a team. Take a look around the nation year after year at the all-conference teams. The vast majority of players making up these teams come from teams at the top of their conferences.

I would be lying to you if I said I did not take great pride in the individual honors I received while playing college basketball at

Kansas State University. It was humbling to receive Big Eight Conference Player of the Year honors in both my junior and senior seasons. However, there is no chance I would have ever been considered for those honors had our team not won the conference championship in both my sophomore and junior years. The notoriety, which led to my personal accolades, was a direct result of our team's success.

Winning teams produce honored individuals. At the same time, winning teams consist of players who focus on making plays for their teammates. If we can get our players to understand the connection that honored individuals are the players who focus on making plays for teammates, then chances are we are going to have a winning team.

Post-game

Leaders must embrace the philosophy of making others look good before anyone else on the team will take ownership of the same philosophy.

As a leader, you must hold yourself accountable for the performance of those on your team. You must be the first one to make plays for your teammates. **If someone on your team has failed, then you have failed as a leader for allowing them to be in the position to fail.** What could you, as the leader, have done to better prepare your teammate to not fail or not allow them to be in the position to fail in the first place?

Live your life everyday looking to make plays for your teammates. What can you do to help make your people look better? Better in the eyes of clients, better in the eyes of other teammates, better in the eyes of vendors and — most importantly — better in the eyes of their friends and family.

Leaders automatically receive individual accolades for success. Triumphant leaders give these accolades back to teammates quickly. The more your teammates see you making plays for others, the quicker they will begin to act in the same manner. Not only will they begin to make plays for their fellow teammates, they will look to make plays for you — their leader.

This is when trust begins to pay dividends for everyone.

There is an old axiom that goes, "It's amazing what a group of people can achieve when nobody is worried about who will get the credit."

It might be fair to add a second part to that truthful saying. "And ultimately, when that team of people is successful, there will be enough praise to go around for everyone involved."

Not Always Right

Pre-game

No one is right all of the time. This is simply human nature.

Understanding this, however, is the key.

The bigger issue when analyzing a decision, which ultimately turns out to be a mistake is, "What motivated that decision?" **Many times the motivating factors of a decision are more telling than the actual decision itself.**

Secure leaders — effective agents of change — will not always be right, but they must always be motivated for the right reasons.

163

Game Time

I am not 100 percent correct all of the time. (And my wife, Barb, reminds me of that often.)

On the court and in our programs, where our teams have enjoyed success throughout the years, I still make my fair share of mistakes. Some of the issues may include playing time, discipline and recruiting decisions.

We feel very strongly about the decisions we make and the reasoning behind those decisions. However, it would be irresponsible for me to believe I never make a mistake.

That is why we try to live by the belief: **"Not always right, but always motivated by the right reasons."**

This simply illustrates that even if we make a mistake, the process for which we made a decision or decisions that led to that mistake must be fair and just. Ultimately, the reasoning for any decision that we make has to have the best intentions in mind for our program, our players, the school and the community.

Of course, any time you have the word "intentions" involved, there is room for error. Now factor in the reality of all of the people the consequences of our decisions impact — players, their families, students, fans, alumni, boosters and more.

There are very few professions that are held as publicly accountable as professional coaching — both fairly and unfairly.

But while we as coaches are judged by many, I believe our ultimate responsibility starts with the parents of our players. In fact, the type of relationship we want to enjoy with our parents is a model for the relationships we want to enjoy with all stakeholders in our program.

Extending a scholarship offer to a young man is doing much more than asking him to come play basketball at your school. You are asking him and his parents for their trust in you. You are asking them to believe you will help to shape this young man into the best person he can be — not simply the best basketball player he can be.

Everyone wants what is best for their child — and understandably so. As coaches, our responsibility is to do what is best for the program while also providing for the individual players.

I always explain to parents our philosophy: "I will treat your son the same way I would want my own son or daughter treated."

As a parent, I know I have not always been correct in every decision that I have made with our children. However, because of my love for and wanting the best for Angie and Kevin, I have been motivated for the right reasons to make those decisions. This has meant telling them "no" or disciplining them at times. It has broken my heart to break their hearts. However, I felt it was the best thing to do for their overall wellbeing.

The same goes for our players. We treat all of our players the way we expect our own sons or daughters to be treated. They have to earn everything they receive and they need to be held accountable for their actions. But, no matter what, we will respect them and love them and all of our decisions will be motivated by the right factors.

It's easier for me to sit across from parents now and understand the decisions they are faced with during the recruitment process. When our son, Kevin, was graduating from high school, I was coaching in the NBA. That meant Kevin would go on to play college ball under someone else.

We wanted an atmosphere that would be nurturing for Kevin yet one that would challenge him and hold him accountable for his actions. Kevin ultimately decided upon Coach Rob Evans' program at Arizona State University, which was nearly 2,000 miles away from our home in Atlanta at the time. However, as parents, Barb and I could not have been more pleased.

We both felt Coach Evans would treat Kevin as his own and that is exactly what happened during Kevin's four years with the program. Not only did Kevin graduate in four years (he redshirted his first season in Tempe), Coach Evans also helped grow Kevin into one of the top guards in the Pac-10 Conference by the end of his junior year.

As many people know, Kevin took advantage of a now defunct NCAA rule (which is often referred to as the "Kevin Kruger Rule") to join our roster at UNLV for his senior season. The rule stated that any athlete who had already earned a degree yet still had a year left of eligibility remaining could transfer to another institution to continue graduate studies without sitting out a season.

However, what many people don't know is that Kevin would have never even considered transferring had Coach Evans not been dismissed by ASU after Kevin's junior year. We put our trust in Coach Evans and gave him our young son who we loved dearly and he delivered! Barb and I will forever be grateful for this.

Our goal is to have all of our parents enjoy the same experience with their sons. We cannot promise that each player will get large amounts of playing time or that each player will turn into a star. But we can promise that each player will receive a fair chance and as much support as possible to become the best that he can be — both on the court and in the classroom.

And, we promise that while every decision we make may not always turn out to be 100 percent correct, all of our decisions will be made for the right reasons.

That is the way any parent should want it — as well as any supporter of the program.

Post-game

Decisions made by leaders impact numerous people. Many times one decision will impact certain team members positively while that same decision will impact another group of team members negatively.

These are the moments that make or break leaders.

Often times "being right" is subjective. Because of this, making such crucial decisions can be hazardous for leaders. Thus, the decision-making process then becomes the most important factor in this entire situation.

As a leader, you must ask yourself, "What is motivating me to make this decision?" **Ultimately, your decision-making process should be consistent and should always come back to what is best for the overall good of the team and its objectives.**

If your decision-making process is grounded in this philosophy, you will maintain the trust of your team members, even when a decision may negatively impact them.

Like parents who want the best for their children, successful leaders want what is best for the people they are leading. However, with their team members' best interests at heart, there is a time to say "no" and there are times to hold team members accountable.

Leaders will always have their decisions questioned. That is part of the job. Effective leaders, however, never give people a reason to question their motives for making such decisions.

Precedents vs. Getting It Right

Pre-game

Disciplining team members is part of a leader's responsibilities. However, the disciplining process is an ongoing process that builds a foundation on a daily basis.

A leader is continuously earning his right to discipline on a case-by-case basis while team members are constantly earning their respective levels of punishment.

Game Time

Our teams do not have many hard and fast rules. A list of rules can back you into a corner.

I disagree with the argument that setting a precedent for players is critical, particularly when dealing with disciplinary issues. We are not interested in setting a precedent. We are interested in getting it right.

Players on our team know what is expected of them. We treat them fairly and base all of our decisions on what is in the best interest of the team. Rules and precedents diminish the opportunity for us to get the most out of each player. Each player has his own unique circumstances that we need to understand to best maximize his potential.

We teach our players to not be concerned with how we treat other people, including other players. They need to trust that our objective is the same with each and every player — to get the most out of him. How we get there with one player may be different with how we get there with another.

An awkward situation arose for us during the 2006–07 season at UNLV. Joel Anthony was a senior center for us that year. During his three years in our program, he improved his play as much as anyone we had ever coached. By the time the NCAA Tournament came around in March, he was one of the top defenders in the nation.

Joel, who had a tremendous mother who was a high school principal in Montreal, was a coach's dream. He worked hard, graduated with good grades and was a selfless teammate. Coaches loved him and his teammates loved him.

That's why it shocked everyone when Joel showed up late for a team meeting during the season. After the meeting, I called Joel aside. "You've put me in an awkward spot here, Joel," I told him.

I could see the pain in Joel's eyes and I heard the hurt in his voice. "I'm sorry, Coach. It will never happen again," he told me. There was no doubt in my mind he was telling the truth.

No punishment that we could have given Joel at this time would hurt more than what he was feeling. He knew he had let his coaches down as well as his teammates and he was willing to do anything he had to do to make it up to us. My discussion with Joel was the last time this incident was discussed. There was no punishment.

Although it was unspoken, Joel spent the rest of the season making up for his one mistake. He was early to every team function and he made it a point to be. He was indebted to us.

Had there been precedents set, things may have not gone the same way. Imagine if a "list of rules" read that if you miss a team meeting you had to sit out a half of a game? This would then be reported in the media. "Joel Anthony will sit out the first half of tonight's game because he broke team rules."

So suddenly, all that Joel worked for over the past two and a half years — including redshirting a year between his junior and senior season for the good of the team — would be tarnished because he would become known as a guy who "broke team rules." What would that do to his confidence?

Some people may say that is playing favorites. We believe it is making the right decision for the correct situation. And, when we make such a decision, we choose a time to address the entire team on why we made the decision we made. As you can imagine, the other players generally get it.

Players earn their own punishment. They know it and we know it.

It's like being a parent. Parents do not punish their kids solely on one bad act. If a child is a good child and she happens to make a mistake, a parent is most likely to be more lenient. However, if she is constantly getting into trouble, the "mistake" is much more likely to lead to a bigger punishment.

In this case, Joel had earned the foundation for our reaction. Had it been a freshman or a player we had experienced issues with in the past, we would have most likely reacted differently. And the disciplinary actions would be whatever that unique situation called for.

The key for us is to treat each member of the team fairly and consistently so as to assist in helping them all achieve their potential as players and people.

Post-game

If you treat your team members fairly and with respect, nothing should change when you are challenged with the situation of disciplining.

Fairness and trustfulness is the foundation of leadership. It is also the foundation of proper discipline. Teams that trust their leaders to be fair during the good times will also trust their leaders to make fair decisions during tougher times.

Setting precedents can be dangerous. Don't make precedents by setting precedents. It can back you into a corner.

Give yourself the freedom to make disciplinary decisions on a case-by-case basis. Be fair and trust yourself.

Communicate to your team how you expect to hold them accountable and how you will decide upon disciplinary actions when necessary. Explain to them how this type of decision-making process protects both them and you.

It will also show your team members you trust them and value them as individuals.

Human Nature vs. Human Nature

Pre-game

Human nature is about **confidence, and confidence can either bring you success or lead you to failure**. It is all about how you address each and every situation with this in mind.

Game Time

As coaches, our greatest ally is human nature. At the same time, our toughest opponent is human nature.

We are determining on almost a weekly basis which side of human nature we are on and how we must adjust.

Many people, observing from afar, tend to take the personal part out of athletics. They assume certain players have certain abilities and that is the level they should always play at regardless of the situation. This couldn't be further from the truth.

The reality is athletes are people. They have good days and weeks and bad days and weeks, just like all of us. And, when you are talking about college age young men like we deal with, there are many variables to consider.

School work. Lack of money. Girlfriend issues. Being away from home. Right or wrong, these types of everyday issues can all potentially impact the performance of a player on the court.

Another thing we find that people tend to forget is that our players are huge fans of our own teams. It is personal, very personal for them whether we win or lose.

Loyal fans may be hurt and disappointed when their team loses, however, they do not have to read about or have to listen to their performance being scrutinized day-in and day-out by others — many times by others you might not categorize as "qualified." It can be a very painful and humiliating experience, especially for a young adult who is still maturing emotionally.

At the same time, players do get to enjoy the fruits of their victories at a greater level than even the most loyal of fans. Others sing their praises and they are adored by supporters. It can be an amazing rush.

Our job is to temper both of these situations by understanding human nature and reacting accordingly.

When a team is on a roll and enjoying success, that team becomes most vulnerable to an upset. Players begin to get more accolades from fans and classmates. Winning becomes the expectation, rather than doing the little things — taking care of the details — that it takes to win. This is all human nature.

As coaches, our job in this situation is to pat our players on the back and tell them they are doing a good job. It is important to keep that confidence up. However, we must continually remind them why they are successful, what it is they are doing effectively and leading to the results of winning ballgames.

Our players need to make this correlation: They are receiving all of this positive feedback not because they are winning but because they are performing in a way that is producing results, which ultimately leads to winning ballgames.

We want them to know why they are winning so they have a chance to do it again.

On the other end of the spectrum is when a player or team is struggling.

Obviously, a player performing below expectations wants to start performing better and begins to battle with pressure. We must find a way to work with him to get his confidence back.

If a shooter is not able to find his range and he is not shooting the ball well, we need him to put in the extra time to work on that skill. It is a commitment, however, because the player is struggling and human nature is pushing him to do something about it. He is usually more than willing to put in the extra work. The external pressure of the judgment of others has a lot to do with this.

As the player puts in the extra time and begins to work on his shot more, he starts getting better results and his confidence begins to rise. Chances are the player will soon bust out of his shooting slump and begin to perform at the level of expectations for him, if not higher.

This is where human nature comes in again. At this point, the player may no longer be feeling the external pressure of failure and may not be driven to put in the extra time to work on his shooting.

Again, as coaches, **it is our responsibility to make a correlation between the actions that led to the results**. We must remind the player after a good game that he experienced those results because he invested the time. It was that time and commitment that caused the success and to repeat the success, he needs to continue that commitment.

Post-game

One of the hardest things for many leaders to do is to have a correct understanding of their teammates when it comes to confidence. This is because high-quality leaders are extremely confident and comfortable with both their strengths and their weaknesses. It can be difficult at times for them to connect with people who do not share that same level of comfort with their strengths, but particularly their weaknesses.

This is why having a firm grasp on human nature is so critical for leaders. Empathetic leadership means you are able to put yourself in the role of your teammates to best understand what they need and consequently how to lead them.

Confidence can lead a teammate to do incredible things to benefit the team; overconfidence can do things that can

179

bring the entire team down. And all is a result of human nature.

As a leader you must know when to go the extra mile to improve someone's confidence or when to strategically guard against someone's confidence getting too high. The best way to accomplish either one of these is to not focus on outcomes — positive or negative — but on what actions or non-actions led to the outcomes.

Human nature encourages us to judge everything purely on success or failure. Meanwhile, strong leadership teaches us to understand why we succeed or why we fail. Continually teach your team this and you will be a great leader.

Making a Habit of It

Pre-game

Make a habit out of creating positive habits for yourself and others.

Success is a day-to-day process and our daily habits have more to do with this than anything else.

No one can change the fact that we are creatures of habit. However, **we do have the power to change our habits and create newer, more positive ones**.

Game Time

On numerous occasions people have told us the thing they like the most about watching our teams play is that if one of our players winds up on the floor and it's a dead ball, his four teammates run over to help him up. They tell us it is something small, but they believe it shows togetherness and teamwork.

We agree. And that is why we coach this act.

Yes, it is actually required of all of our players to make sure they help up a teammate who has hit the floor. In fact, we review this during our film sessions. If we see on film a player is not making an effort to get to the fallen teammate and help him up at a dead ball, that player will be held accountable.

Some people may question whether this has anything at all to do with actually winning games. We believe it does.

It is all part of creating habits. **As coaches, that is our job — to be habit creators for our players.** People, including athletes, are creatures of habit. While we cannot change that fact, we can work to alter the actual habits of our players.

Helping someone off of the floor is representative of so many other things that are important in a team setting. It helps to build the culture within a program to always be there for a teammate and to pick a teammate up when he is down.

Unfortunately, this type of culture does not exist in all team settings.

At times, players may come to us with habits already existing that are not consistent with the type of work ethic or philosophy that we expect in our program. Thus, we work to find ways to alter habits, which is not easy. However, repetition is the key. If a player does something enough times, he begins to do it unconsciously — by simple habit. This is the goal.

Because of this, we require the same from our players in practice as we expect from them in a game. It may appear odd to an observer to see nine guys rushing to pick someone up during one of our practices. However, that is what they may see. One of the worst things that we can do as coaches is to allow things to happen in practice that we do not want to happen in games, or to expect things to happen in games that we do not require to happen in practice.

If a player takes a shot in practice that we do not want him to take in a game, he needs to hear about it immediately in practice. If he does not hear about it in practice and he takes that same shot in a game, then we as coaches are accountable for the shot, not the player.

In sports, habits are created in practice. The games themselves are ultimately where the habits are exhibited publicly.

There are several drills that we run in practice that are designed to build simple habits.

We have found over the years that many players can be sloppy with layups because they do not concentrate fully on the simple shot. In a game, a missed layup is one of the worst things a team can have happen. You cannot allow yourself to be in a position for two easy points and not convert.

We put such an important emphasis on this that we run a simple drill that is developed to help our players create the habit of focusing on layups and not taking them for granted. In the timed drill, the only layups that count are the layups that hit the backboard and go directly through the net — without hitting any rim.

It sounds basic and it is. However, it helps to create a key habit for our players. Now when our players have a chance for a simple layup, our goal is to have habit take over. They now have a habit of picking out a point on the board and laying the ball up easy — without thinking about it.

On the court and off the court, our goal is to help our players develop positive habits that will last them a lifetime. Some are easy and some are much more difficult, but any positive habit will pay dividends for years to come.

Post-game

A leader needs to be a habit expert. Not only must he have a full understanding of his own habits, both positive and negative, he must have a strong understanding of the habits of his team members.

With this information he must do two things. First, he must use the information about current habits to put his team members in the best position possible for them to succeed. Secondly, he must identify habits that should be created for individuals and work with team members to try and create those habits.

Simply telling a team member "you need to develop this habit" is not enough. In fact, if that is your expectation then you have failed as a leader. **The most effective leaders work with their team members to help them create the habits they need to be successful in their roles.**

Leaders of substance understand the importance of creating habits for their team members and, more importantly, are willing to invest the time into helping their team members create the respective habits.

Sometimes these habits are big, but many times they are small in the eyes of employees — even if those habits have a big impact on the organization. For example, in many professional service companies, team members don't enjoy the simple process of tracking billable hours. It can be deemed as tedious work to some employees and they may view it as busy work that actually removes them from completing customer service related tasks. However, if hours are not logged efficiently and effectively, it can lead to serious financial issues for the company.

Helping employees to value the habit of being on top of their billable hours may seem simple to most leaders, but it cannot be overlooked. It must be addressed on a continual basis and, in fact, leaders must take responsibility to make sure even the most simple of tasks become habit for their team members.

The entire process requires a great deal of patience. However, the payoff of creating positive habits for individuals on your team means a stronger and more efficient team, which produces better results.

Be consistent in reinforcing good actions and habits frequently while also addressing poor actions and habits in the same matter. The correlation of good/poor habits with good/poor results is the key to this communication.

Picture the Results

Pre-game

An action should not be made without anticipating and preparing for the possible reactions.

Because many of the decisions we must make are almost instantaneous, **constantly picturing the results of our actions will help us develop the habit of making positive choices on a consistent basis.**

And, also understand that making the right decision is habitual.

Game Time

I am always intrigued to watch people diagram plays. Not necessarily to see what they are doing with the offensive players, but to see what they are doing with the defensive players.

Do they put the defender right up on the offensive player? On the weak side, where do they envision the defensive man to be or, more importantly, where are they telling their players to envision the defensive man to be?

Diagramming an offensive play involves much more than telling all five of your players where to move. We want them to understand the different places the defenders may be, the options of how the defenders will probably act and the rhythm in which we want to run the play to be the most effective.

Our players can only learn to understand all of this if they are able to picture the results of their own actions. We don't want them to look at the Xs and Os on the dry erase board and simply emulate the movement we draw up. We want them to actually visualize what should happen and what could happen so they are familiar with the possible scenarios.

They cannot be thinking, "I am supposed to move there now." We want them thinking, "When X happens, I am supposed to move there so Y will happen. If that does not happen, I should do this."

A basketball game — much like life — is an ongoing exercise of controlled spontaneity. We can only prepare our players so much for something that might happen on the floor. If we have done our duty as coaches, we have prepared our players for the different scenarios that they may be faced with and they will not have to think so much as instinctively react.

For example, if we want to run a particular play and have only practiced that set against a man-to-man defense, we can't expect our players to be prepared to run the same set flawlessly against a zone. It is our responsibility to teach them about the different obstacles they may face and then prepare them on how to best face those respective obstacles.

At some point, however, they are on their own to perform and implement what they have been taught. If they have done their preparation and have pictured the results of their actions, they are much more likely to make the right decisions and deliver positive results.

We are constantly preaching to our players, "Picture the results of your actions." This, of course, is an even more important habit to possess off the basketball court.

On Fridays, at the end of the practice, we will reiterate this to our guys. "If you are out with a buddy tonight and someone who's drunk starts to mess with your buddy, what are you going to do?" I may ask the team. "Are you going to 'have his back' and try to prove yourself, or are you going to get your buddy and leave?"

Our players need to picture this situation in their minds so that if this does happen, they are familiar with the correct decision and that decision becomes a habit.

A wrong decision made in a split-second can change a life forever, let alone the course of a basketball game.

Post-game

People who are in leadership positions tell their teams to do something.

Strong leaders communicate with their teams about what it is they want to accomplish, how they are going to try to accomplish the feat, and what can be expected along the way. This helps team members to picture the results of their actions.

Strong teams are built because the team members become more efficient and effective as individuals working within the framework of the team. These team members grow when they begin to picture the results of their actions as they develop the skill of providing themselves with feedback on their own actions.

As an effective leader, you have already set the expectations for what members of your team should expect from their actions. If these are not the results the team member is producing, he will alter his actions in an effort to produce those expected results.

Make it a habit to teach your team members how to picture their results. If you can accomplish this, your team will make it a habit of choosing the right decisions without you even having to be involved.

Making Progress

Pre-game

When the objective is to maximize your team's potential, simply being pleased with a win is not enough.

The environment a win produces for a team must be used as a tool for making further progress. **Top tier teams build upon each and every win and use the positive environment created by winning to continue to progress.**

There is no better time to improve as a team and as individuals than immediately after enjoying a success.

Game Time

Timing is everything. And we're not talking about running an offensive set.

The best opportunity to make significant improvements with individuals or an entire team is coming off a victory. In fact, more progress can be made after a win than after a loss.

Why? Because of timing.

Most fans would probably believe the opposite to be true. But think about this in terms of your own family relationships. Are there better times to give constructive feedback to someone you care about?

You can say the exact same thing to the same person in the same tone. However, depending upon the situation, the person you are giving the constructive feedback to is going to receive the information differently. If he is coming off of a negative situation, he is much more likely to be offended by the suggestion. However, if he is coming off of a positive situation, he is going to be more open to the feedback and will most likely respond positively to it.

The same can be said with athletes. **There are just some things you can say to players after good games that you cannot tell them after bad games.** Not because you are pandering to them, but because you need to protect their confidence.

If a player's confidence is already shaken, you don't want to add an additional burden to the player by going too far with your feedback.

At the same time, if the player is performing at a high level and the team is winning, there are always areas for improvement. As coaches, our responsibility is to not let our players settle. We must challenge them to improve upon their weaknesses now to avoid defeats later in the season.

There is a reason teams go on winning streaks. Good coaches with strong leaders on their rosters take advantage of the winning environment and help their teams improve while still winning. They leverage the confidence that is produced by winning ballgames with constructive feedback, thus, bettering their players and their teams for the long run.

Unfortunately, this type of leveraging is not possible when a team is losing because of the lack of confidence. At this point, coaches must work to not only help the players improve, but build the team's confidence as well. (This reality is one of the main reasons why NBA winning franchises keep winning and why losing NBA franchises find it difficult to change.)

One of the biggest mistakes a team can make is not trying to better itself while it is experiencing success. This is the opportune time to grow as a team . . . and individuals.

Superior teams increase their focus during

winning streaks and become elite teams. Average or poor teams enjoy the winning while it lasts, but do not improve themselves for the future.

So the next time you see a team on a long winning-streak, chances are there is much more to that streak than simply momentum. The team is probably making progress each and every day and reaping the benefits.

Post-game

The best leaders understand there is no better environment for teaching and learning than a winning environment.

Teams and individuals currently enjoying success are much more likely to make progress in areas of improvement than teams and individuals who are struggling. Thus, strong leaders take advantage of positive environments by pushing their team members to improve when times are good. Of course, this progress tends to lead to more success.

A strong leader is able to keep her focus on the top priority — having her team perform to its maximum potential. Even though success may come, progress must continue to occur for the team to ultimately reach its main goal of maximizing its potential.

It's not that good leaders are never satisfied. It's simply good leaders know when to use a team's confidence to its greatest advantage.

LESSON TWENTY-NINE

One Loss Cannot Lead to Another

Pre-game

Failure is a cycle that must be detoured.

One bad shot should not lead to another bad shot. And, more importantly, one loss should not lead to another loss. **The negative outcome of one game should not negatively influence the outcome of the next.**

Yes, all losses hurt — some more than others. However, it's how our teams react to those losses that will determine how close we can come to maximizing our potential.

Game Time

We suffered what we consider our toughest loss ever as coaches during our Sweet 16 season with UNLV in 2006–07. We were playing an early season conference game at Wyoming, which is a difficult place to win.

The game started on a down note as our starting senior point guard, my son Kevin, was injured during the first two minutes of the game and would not return. Despite the setback, our team battled and led for most of the game before Wyoming tied the score with under a minute to go.

We had the ball out of bounds and the shot clock was off. We put the ball in the hands of sophomore guard Wink Adams, one of our best ball handlers, finishers and foul shooters (especially with the game on the line).

Everything worked as we had hoped. As Wink drove the lane during the final seconds, he was hacked — not once, but twice. He would be going to the free throw line and we were confident he would hit at least one of the foul shots to allow us to escape with a victory. But then we were stunned to realize that no foul had been called on the play.

Our team was devastated. At that moment, we tried to get the guys ready for overtime and move on as quickly from the situation as possible. But we were fighting human nature and momentum and did not respond well.

We never led during overtime and ended up losing 86–76. We left Wyoming dejected. It was a long, quiet bus ride to the airport and a silent flight home.

On video, the non-foul was even more apparent than in person. We wound up receiving apologies from several people in the days following the loss. While we appreciated the fact the mistake was acknowledged, it actually made the hurt a bit stronger.

However, we had to move on immediately. As coaches, no matter how bad a loss stings, it is our responsibility to make sure the team moves on. Players will respond to how we as coaches respond. And because we were at a crossroads in our season, it was more significant now than ever.

For the first time in many years, UNLV was making waves on the national scene. We were in our third season with the Runnin' Rebels and had started the year 14–2.

The tough Wyoming loss marked the first time all season we had dropped two games in a row (four days earlier we had lost a close game on the road at nationally ranked Air Force) and we were about to see what our team was made of.

It was imperative at this juncture that the loss at Wyoming did not cost us any other games. It is unacceptable for teams to allow one loss to lead to another loss. However, the possibilities of that happening are always there. And because the Wyoming loss was so devastating, we knew it would be even more of a challenge.

When we came back together for practice the following day, our way of handling the missed call was simple — we did not even discuss it. There would be no benefit in us discussing a situation that was out of our control. We wanted to remove our team from the negative as quickly as possible. However, because media members and fans were talking about the bad call, it made our task more difficult.

We simply focused on what we always focus on after a game — what we did well to produce results and what we needed to do better to produce better results.

There was a renewed sense of urgency now because of the two losses, but we used that to our advantage. Our players used that practice and the following practices to focus completely on competing for results. **The missed call was never discussed and our attention went directly to preparing for our next game.** We felt good about where we were collectively as a team.

Externally, however, people were worried. We had just lost two games in a row to drop to 2–2 in conference, Kevin was going to be out for an indefinite period of time with a deep thigh bruise, and a strong BYU team and a competitive San Diego State squad were up next at our place. I'm sure it was safe to say some thought our run was about to end.

In fact, it was only the beginning. Not only did we take care of BYU at home, we followed that game with four more victories to win seven of our first nine conference games. That set us up for our Mountain West Conference Tournament title as well as our two victories in the NCAA Tournament.

The Wyoming loss would mark the only time all season we lost back-to-back games. And although you could make the argument that the loss cost us a share of the regular season title (we finished in second by just one game), it proved to be a pivotal moment in the development of our team.

We did not let one loss — even one that hurt that much — lead to any more defeats. In fact, we learned from the experience. It made us a better team down the stretch as we now had the confidence that we could overcome great obstacles if we continued to concentrate on competing for results and not purely the outcome.

Post-game

We have all had our bad days at work.

Lost a client. Failed to close a deal. Did not meet expectations on a project. Missed sales numbers.

Business is like sports. You will not win every game. **The key to being successful, however, is how you react to failure.**

As a leader, your responsibility is to help your team and team members recover from failure as quickly as possible and grow from the experience. Many of us tend to spend a great portion of our time after a failure rationalizing why we failed and harping upon variables that were out of our control. While there are times external variables do play major roles in our failure, it does not benefit us to focus on them and it definitely does not help us "play the next play."

The first step in moving forward from failure is admitting fault and taking ownership of the unsuccessful results. Only from this point will you be able to identify which variables — those you do have control of — led to the negative situation. Once these have been identified, you can then create a plan that will allow you to positively address those areas and make improvement.

The quicker you and your team can be moving forward and growing in a proactive manner, the further your team will be removed from the negative environment. Then as growth occurs with your team, the confidence lost by the failure will begin to return. This is when your team is past the recovery stage from the failure.

It is important to remember that people outside of your team may dwell on failure for a longer period of time than your team will. You cannot allow this potential negative feedback to impact the confidence of your recovering team.

The biggest winners in sports and business all lose at times. What separates them from the rest is how quickly and proactively they move on from their losses. They never allow one loss to be the cause of another loss.

Be Great Everyday

Pre-game

Consistently performing at a high level is the key to maximizing our potential as both individuals and as teams.

The top performers in any field are typically the people who excel at what they do on a day-to-day basis, not just in crucial situations. These leaders understand that their daily performances have a great impact on others around them.

If we want to be great at something, we must challenge ourselves to be great everyday at whatever it is we are trying to master. Not only will we perform at a level closer to our maximum potential, those around us will also perform at a higher level because of the security we will offer.

Game Time

So much about the game of college basketball takes place away from the court on game day. A team develops its character in such places as the weight room, the practice gym, classes and even on bus and plane rides.

As team leaders emerge throughout this process, they bring with them a sense of security for the rest of the team. This security allows other players to relax and be confident the leader will always be able to give them direction in times of need on and off the court.

While that security is comforting for the rest of the team, it can be a great burden for the leaders themselves. Why? Because true leaders are not called upon to only be great during challenging moments, they are called upon to be great everyday. This is what separates good players from great leaders.

Great leaders understand the impact of their own actions on the entire team and take ownership of that responsibility daily.

When we look back on some of our most successful teams throughout the years, they share similar traits. One of the most important traits is that those teams improved on a daily basis throughout their respective seasons. Much of this can be attributed to the leaders who emerged during those runs.

Players like Steve Henson at Kansas State, Craig Brown at Florida, Matt Heldman at Illinois, and Kevin Kruger at UNLV set the tone for our teams while offering security to the other players.

Every single practice, these players took the floor and practiced to be great. Not just for themselves, but for their teammates. They understood the importance of setting the standard of working to be great every single day and they also understood that they had complete control over this effort.

No player has the ability to make every single shot he takes or successfully defend his opponent every single trip down the court, but he does have the ability to practice and play with maximum effort each and every day.

If a team leader is setting this tone for our team daily, our team will improve immensely throughout that season.

Unfortunately, not every team has a great leader emerge to lead it. As coaches, it is our responsibility to help nurture these potential leaders throughout their time in our program. Some players come more naturally to it, while others have to work more at it. And, the truth is, some will never fit that role. It is a special role for a select few.

As we first wrote this lesson, our program had a possible emerging leader in guard Wink Adams.

Going into his junior season, we knew if Wink chose to do so, he could become one of the top leaders our program has ever had. That was possible because he was already so highly respected by his teammates.

Wink has been a big part of the foundation of what we are doing here at UNLV as he committed to us as a highly respected player out of Houston as part of our first recruiting class.

After averaging over 10 points per game as a freshman reserve, Wink started all 37 games his sophomore year (the only player on the team that season to start every game) as the only non-senior starter on our Sweet 16 squad.

He entered his junior year as a preseason all conference selection and, more importantly, was known for his lockdown defense. In fact, as a freshman Wink tied UNLV's all time record for steals in a game with eight one night against Colorado State.

Entering his third season with us, he had a decision to make. Did he want to embrace the role of being the team leader, the guy who works hard to be great every day?

It was an incredible opportunity for Wink to be around several hardworking upperclassmen his first two seasons, guys like Lou Amundson, Joel Anthony and Kevin. However, it was also very safe because they offered him security.

Entering his third year in the program, others were now looking to him for direction. And that added much more pressure for him.

When we watched film, if someone drove by him to the hole, it became a much bigger deal than it would be just one year before. In practice, if he had a lapse or was not giving his maximum effort, other people were noticing.

Wink was no longer just performing for himself, he was performing for others at all times — both in games and in practice.

Not all players are comfortable with this role. No matter what their personal make up, it is a tough adjustment. However, Wink accepted the challenge head on. His junior year he helped lead us to 27 wins, another conference tournament title and into the second round of the NCAA Tournament. In our final game of the season (a loss against eventual national champion Kansas), Wink delivered one of the most courageous performances of his career and kept us in the game with the Jayhawks for the first 30 minutes.

Now, entering his senior season, the stakes are raised for him. Because of his acceptance as a team leader who strives to be great everyday, the expectations of him by his teammates and fans will be higher his final season. We are confident Wink will deliver.

As with our experience with Wink, trying to help players grow into team leaders can be gratifying for us as coaches. It does not work every time exactly how we want it to, but all of the young men who are confronted with this challenge learn skills that will help them throughout their lives away from basketball.

The goal of being great is too vague for leaders. The goal must be to be great everyday.

Post-game

Effective leaders not only strive to be great every single day, they also help to nurture others to be great every day as well.

This starts through personal effort. We have the ability each and every day to give our maximum possible effort towards whatever it is we are doing at that moment. That is under our complete control.

In a leadership position, we are never performing solely for ourselves. Our team's wellbeing is dependent upon our daily effort and, as leaders, we must fully embrace this understanding as well as accept the challenge. If we do this and give our maximum effort everyday, we create a secure environment in which our teammates can prosper.

Our responsibility as leaders is to identify team members who possess the traits to emerge into fellow leaders. Informal leadership from a teammate is many times as important as formal leadership from a "superior."

The best leaders — formal "superiors" — you will find are those who can help to nurture informal leadership from within teams. These leaders realize the value of peer leadership and work to align the peer leadership with their own leadership values.

When peer leadership is aligned with the values of the "superior" leader, teams move forward successfully. When peer leadership is not aligned with the values of the "superior" leader, teams are at risk of fracturing.

In basketball, you hear the analogy that "it is like having a coach on the floor." And, as a coach, there is nothing more important to a team.

Who on your team is your coach on the floor and, like you, is striving to be great everyday? If you are having a problem answering that, chances are you have not taken the time to nurture someone along.

Remember, great leaders develop other great leaders.

Sunday Nights

Pre-game

Constantly improving the starting point is a key element to being successful. However, **it's crucial that we identify starting points on a consistent basis to help us measure our progress**.

Sometimes these starting point opportunities are as simple as a relaxing Sunday night meal and conversation. It may not seem like much, but come Monday morning, it begins to offer results.

Game Time

One of the most critical aspects of us establishing the culture we wanted during our first three years with UNLV originated from us simply addressing a problem.

When we took over the program we inherited a few players who had the habit of driving back home to California nearly every Saturday night — even during the season (as the team was off on Sundays). Unfortunately, this could lead to many different situations.

Our utmost concern was for the safety of the players. Some would choose to drive back into Las Vegas late Sunday or early Monday without proper rest. The three to four hour trip to Las Vegas from Southern California can be a dangerous one if the driver is not fully alert or is rushing.

We also knew this could lead to missed early Monday morning classes, something that is unacceptable to us. Thus, we created a process that would eliminate this problem — a mandatory Sunday night meeting with the team every week during the school year.

But what started as a solution to a problem quickly grew into so much more. Those meetings have actually become the foundation of each of our player's weeks at UNLV. It allows the entire team to come together to begin each week at the same starting point.

After an informal team meal, we go over

our schedule for the week — when we are running, lifting, practicing, game times and any travel times. Our players are each responsible for developing a weekly planner. They will have all of their classes outlined two weeks ahead of time so we can discuss any possible situations that may arise and do any planning that needs to be done to help them honor their commitments in the classroom.

By doing this on a weekly basis, we take away the opportunity for excuses. There is no chance they will miss an announcement about a practice time or when a team bus is leaving. All of the players are given the information at the same time and they help to hold one another accountable.

But more than that, it helps everyone on the entire team — including me — to regroup entering a new week and find our starting point together. We all know what we have to accomplish each and every day as individuals to be successful as a unit. We also know that in exactly one week, we are going to come back together in the same positive setting and we will hold one another accountable if we have to.

Players live their lives with Sunday night in mind. They know what they have to do after the recently passed Sunday and they know what they have to do to prepare for the next Sunday. It has become part of their foundation.

Our hope as coaches is that this mechanism will help teach our players the important skill set of planning and prioritizing that they will use to help them be successful for the rest of their lives.

Post-game

Sometimes teams just need to check in together and make sure everyone is on the same page.

It's easy as a leader to want to use every opportunity a team is together to push for results. However, every meeting of a team can't be the toughest, most-productive session of the year.

If you are working to improve your team's starting point, be sure you are helping your team to properly identify starting points by which to measure. This must not only be done clearly but it must be done consistently.

Many managers can deem housekeeping meetings as unimportant. But leaders understand the value. **Team members seek consistent delivery of expectations, feedback and other information they believe will help them do their jobs better.**

Be upbeat and on-point during these meetings — don't waste anyone's time. However, be consistent in helping to clearly identify short-term expectations for the team and individuals.

Set a routine schedule that allows you to identify starting points for your team and hold everyone accountable to honoring that schedule — especially yourself.

Accelerate Through Impact

Pre-game

Success is about confidence. While confidence alone does not make you successful, it's what you are able to accomplish with the confidence that leads to success.

Confidence allows you to focus on what needs to be accomplished rather than focusing on what negative outcomes might occur. Too many of us concern ourselves with the fear of failure and, ultimately, this fear begins to dictate our actions.

On the other hand, being confident enables us to perform actions at our highest levels possible. At the point of greatest impact, we accelerate our actions because of our high confidence rather than decelerating because of a lack of confidence.

Accelerating through impact leads to positive results in almost anything we do.

Game Time

Growing up in a house full of brothers, we played sports year round — baseball, basketball, football. This love for all sports comes from Dad.

However, like most former school-aged athletes, my participation in sports eventually became limited to golf. Golf is a great game because it teaches you so much about yourself. It challenges you mentality and also exposes your true character.

Golf is also a perfect example of one of the most fundamental rules for success in almost any sport — accelerating through impact.

When striking the ball, do you accelerate through your club's impact with the ball or do you decelerate? This one detail is critical. You will find that topnotch golfers always accelerate through the ball, thus, generating more power. Typically, golfers who play at a lower level tend to decelerate their swings.

What is the biggest difference between these two types of players? Confidence.

The best golfers are so confident in their swings and where the ball is going to go that they are not worried about the many possible negative outcomes of accelerating through impact with the ball. They are confident the ball will go straight so they are simply concerned with hitting the ball well.

On the other hand, golfers who lack this confidence tend to decelerate at impact in an effort to avoid the negative outcomes of a ball that might be well struck but heading in a bad direction. Unfortunately, this deceleration leads to other problems with the swing.

Not only is accelerating through impact important for a golf swing, it's crucial for many actions in almost any sport — a pitcher throwing a baseball or a batter swinging the bat, a running back hitting the hole in football, a volleyball player spiking the ball for a kill, a basketball player shooting a jump shot.

In all cases, the athlete should look to accelerate through the moment of impact to better increase his or her chances of success.

However, being able to accelerate through impact is not as easy as simply saying, "I am confident."

A person's confidence is directly correlated to his investment of time for preparation. The more prepared a person is, the more confident he will be.

Again, look at the example of the two golfers. The topnotch golfer has spent countless

217

hours on the driving range with his golf clubs in his hands. This preparation allows him the confidence to know he will hit the ball where he wants to hit it.

The poor golfer has not made this same type of time commitment and lacks the confidence because of a lack of preparation.

As coaches, we need our players to play with a high level of confidence at all times. This confidence, however, can only be generated if our players are prepared to face the challenges that lie ahead of them. Preparing them for this takes a large investment of time.

This is one reason why senior players are so valuable at the college level. Underclassmen, many times, are the more talented players in college basketball. However, by the time players are seniors, many of them have already faced so many different challenges that they are better prepared for most situations. They are more confident in what needs to be done and are able to accelerate through the moment of impact at key parts of the game.

Our objective for advancing younger players in their preparation is to put them in situations in practice that are similar to those they will face in games and to have them enjoy success in that environment. That success, which comes from investing their time in preparation, begins to translate into confidence.

We also need to make sure our players

grow from unsuccessful experiences as well. If we lose a close game on the road, we must learn from the situation so the players will be more comfortable the next time we are in a hostile environment with the game on the line. Again, time is needed for positive preparation.

Playing timid in all sports is a recipe for disaster. Playing with confidence is the key to success. However, only through making an investment of time to be mentally and physically prepared can an athlete play with the highest level of confidence and feel comfortable when it is time to accelerate through the moment of impact.

Post-game

Do you have the chance at a new key account? A big presentation to a current client? Hitting a revenue goal for the first time?

These are all moments of impact we may face in our careers.

There are two things we must remember to help us accelerate through these moments of impact.

First, make the time commitment to be prepared. Stress the importance of this to members of your team. It's easy in organizations to let the day-to-day issues get in the way of properly planning and preparing for big moments of impact.

219

The more prepared you and your team are for the big pitch or the big presentation, the more confident you will be. You must personally value this time for preparation or else your team will not value it either.

Second, accelerate fully through the entire moment of impact. Many sales organizations are strong at delivering an initial presentation but do not follow-up in an effective or timely manner. A strong presentation is wasted if the follow-up process is weak and the deal is not closed.

Another example of accelerating through impact in business is when your organization is almost to the point of turning the corner or reaching a new level. As a leader of this organization, if you see you are close to reaching that goal, now is not the time to coast. Now is the time to focus on the details that are allowing you to be successful and accelerate fully through that moment of impact.

Make the time investment to be fully prepared, be confident and accelerate through the moment of impact. That is a recipe for success in almost anything we do.

Slow Down

Pre-game

A temptation in basketball is to do everything as fast as possible. Basketball is a game played at a quick pace and with continuous spontaneity.

However, **activity does not equate to productivity and we continually remind our players to "slow down."** In fact, "slow down" may be the term our players hear from us more than any other term throughout the season.

Game Time

Over the past 25 years, we've had teams that have walked the ball up the court as well as teams that have liked to get out and run. No matter the style of play, however, our message has been consistent — slow down.

There is a myth in basketball as well as most sports that playing hard and with a high level of intensity means having to play fast at all times. Playing only with intensity does not guarantee productivity and, as coaches, we are focused on production.

This is especially difficult for our younger players, particularly point guards who are handling the ball more often. The college game is much quicker, more physical and played with more intensity than even the highest level of high school or AAU basketball and it takes an adjustment period.

Usually the game begins to move so quickly that the younger players try to match that speed. Unfortunately, that is when everything becomes a blur to them.

Instead of trying to speed up to match the increased speed, the players should be doing just the opposite — slowing down. **When you slow down on the court, things begin to develop more clearly in your mind.** You start to see openings and opportunities you never saw before as well as allowing you the opportunity to pick your spots more effectively.

Slowing down also allows a young player to concentrate on doing things he feels comfortable doing. Once he does this and experiences some success, his confidence grows, which helps his all-around game.

During our 2006–07 Sweet 16 season at UNLV, we had a point guard tandem that were polar opposites when it came to experience. My son, Kevin, was our starting senior while Marcus Lawrence, a true freshman out of Las Vegas, was the backup.

A few games into league play, Kevin suffered a leg injury that kept him out of five crucial games, meaning Marcus was called on to fill the big shoes of a senior team leader during an important stretch of the season.

We went 5–0 in the five games Marcus started during that period — including key wins over BYU and San Diego State. But the key to Marcus' performance wasn't about what he did do — it was about what he didn't do. He didn't turn the ball over and he didn't allow the guy he was guarding to be productive.

Marcus was put in a position to emphasize the parts of his game that he was very comfortable with, ball handling and defense. Kevin was a scorer and if we had asked that of Marcus at the time, I'm sure we all would have been frustrated in the results. Instead, Marcus was able to enjoy success in areas where he excelled and his confidence grew. His defense and point guard play off the bench ended up being an important part of our post season run. That's not something you hear often about a true freshman point guard.

We believe the key to Marcus' success was his preparation. He knew what to expect and what was expected of him. Often times, you will see players or teams rush because of a lack of preparation. Things are moving so quickly and they are not prepared for it, so they go as fast as they can, trying to cut corners, just to catch up.

Teams need to be ready. They need to know what to expect and when the game begins to move quickly, they need to have the confidence in their preparation to allow the plan to work without worrying about rushing.

One thing we continuously stress to our players on offense is "Wait." Yes, wait. Wait a few moments before putting the play into motion or making your cut. The defensive player is anticipating immediate movement from you. The longer you wait, the more nervous he will become or you have the opportunity to lull him to sleep. He knows you are going to do something, but he doesn't know when.

We want efficient movement, not rapid movement. As is the case with any sport, a change of pace is effective in basketball. We want to vary our speeds and not simply go full speed ahead at all times.

Post-game

Many business leaders and entrepreneurs wind up being the victims of their own success.

Rapid advances in technology have increased the speed that we believe we must do business. And, as a leader, the demand for your time becomes greater and greater with the more success you achieve.

Put the two of these factors together and at some point, working harder or putting in more hours are no longer viable options. This is when you need to do something you may not feel comfortable doing — slow down.

Start with a simple exercise. Look at your calendar or the projects you are personally accountable for at this moment. Are there any appointments you don't truly need to have or are there projects you should be delegating? If the answer is yes, and it probably is, do something about it. Chances are if you are so busy, you are not doing many of the things you are responsible for at the highest level either, and this will eventually catch up to you.

Slowing down is not solely about improving your quality of life although that is an important aspect. No, **this is also a productivity audit**. Who or what does your intense schedule negatively impact?

Your family? Current clients? The environment at your office? If you are so busy day-to-day, who is addressing the overall strategic vision for your team?

The game of life is played at an intense speed and it is only increasing. Be prepared for it. Take the time to have a plan and then have confidence in what you do the best and do it at your own pace and without cutting corners.

Don't be active just for the sake of being active. Be productive by slowing down. The production will show in your bottom-line.

Always Have Their Backs

Pre-game

No one wants to make a mistake in front of 18,000 people. Or have their failures or shortcomings highlighted on television, in the morning paper or discussed on talk radio.

Just and sometimes unjust, that's part of the pressure of being a collegiate or professional athlete.

That is why **it is crucial the players know we coaches will always have their backs.**

This doesn't mean we condone all of their actions and it does not mean we do not get frustrated ourselves when players are not doing what needs to be done — both on and off the court — for them to be in a position to perform at the highest level. What it means is that we will always be there to support them.

And sometimes we are the only ones doing that.

Game Time

Our job as coaches is to develop an atmosphere that will allow our players to maximize their potential. This ideal atmosphere is one where players are comfortable enough to focus internally on the team and not on external factors regarding the team.

To do this we must protect the team and our players from as much negative exposure as possible. We must also serve as the biggest promoters of our players when good things occur.

Doing this effectively means when there is blame to be taken, we — the coaches — must shoulder that blame. However, when there is praise to be given, our players need to get it all.

We understand the media outlets that cover our team are an important part of this process. Our players are arguably the biggest fans of our program. This is a fact that can be overlooked by most sports fans, but it is crucial that we keep this in mind. And things have become even more difficult in this area with the growing popularity of chat rooms and message boards, which many people use for their own personal agendas without accountability.

What is being said in the media is being heard and read by our players and it could, potentially, undermine what we are trying to do as a team. That's why a staple of our program has been how we have decided to work with the media. We have made a conscious decision to always remain positive when dealing with reporters. This both protects our players when things are not going positively as well as allows us the opportunity to promote individual players publicly when it is deserved.

By having this standard when dealing with the media, we gain trust internally. Our players have the comfort of knowing that we will not dwell upon negative issues through the media, and that we will exclusively deal with these internally. And, if something is taken out of context and used negatively in a media outlet, we have a track record with our players. They trust that we will have their backs publicly and we are able to negate issues that might arise from such negative stories or reports.

This mentality also carries over into game situations.

I have only received five or six technical fouls in my entire coaching career and I like to think each one was deserved because I actually wanted to receive them for calculated reasons. Basically, these were all to show support to a player or the team by letting them know we understood their frustration.

While most technicals are based on a single incident in a single game, sometimes a coach may have a bigger plan in mind if, indeed, he wants to send a message to a player or players to let them know he is with them.

During our time with the Atlanta Hawks, we had a situation such as this occur involving Dikembe Mutombo, the well known All Star center. Deke, as we called him, is a good and caring individual and plays with a lot of emotion.

One game Deke was getting quite frustrated with the officiating and you could see him getting more and more emotional about it as the game went on. Basically, he felt helpless.

Finally, after another call went against him — even though it was arguably the right call — Deke showed a little more emotion than the referee, David Jones, preferred and Deke got called for a technical foul. His frustration was boiling over and it was time for us to show we had his back.

Out of earshot from any players, I asked Dave, whom I had known for a few years, to "T" me up. He understood exactly what I was after and promptly gave me the technical, my first as a head coach in the NBA.

The entire team saw the support their teammate received. More importantly, all of the players appreciated it, particularly Deke. As the free throws were being shot, he walked up to me, looked down at me and said two simple words. "Thanks, Coach."

It's all we needed to hear.

Post-game

In reality, the customer is not always right. It's hard to think this way sometimes when jobs are on the line and you need to hit numbers, either for quarterly reports or for pure cash-flow reasons.

It's easy in businesses for clients or even upper management to want to blame others in your organization for problems that they themselves may actually be causing. And, many times, it's easy as a leader to blame our own team members rather than holding others accountable for their end of the bargain.

You have to have the backs of the people you are leading even if it sometimes puts you in an uncomfortable situation.

Your followers have to see you support them and believe that you want them to succeed. Without this, your ability to lead is nullified.

Once the members of the team you are leading understand you have their backs, their loyalty to you will be greatly enhanced and they will begin to do anything they can to: 1) not let you down; and 2) try to make you look good.

It's the give and take of leadership. You give your people your full support and then you are able to take advantage of their loyalty to you. This type of relationship is built on trust and if either a team member or a leader is not sincere, then it will not work.

If you are building a team, find people you trust and move forward supporting them and protecting them every step of the way.

Play Who You Trust

Pre-game

When deciding what players should be in the game at different times, it's not always about which guy is the best athlete, or who the best shooter is, or who is the most popular in the eyes of the fans. **We play who we trust.** And that is particularly true when the game is on the line.

Who you trust may not always be apparent by looking at the stat sheet. Instead, you see your players day-in and day-out both on and off the court and you know what they are made of.

You know whom you would want in the trenches with you, who the fighters are. Those are the guys you put your trust in when it's crunch time. You put the game in their hands and, more often than not, they will repay you for doing that.

Game Time

Curtis Terry was a junior on our 2006–07 UNLV team. He played in all 37 games that season while playing four different positions — everything except for center. While he never started a game for us that year, he was on the court at the end in many of those games.

He wasn't the quickest guy or the best shooter but he always found a way to positively impact the game and we wanted him on the floor during the final moments of contests. He hounded his man on defense and on offense he would make his teammates better and hit a shot when needed. Simply put, he was a gamer. In fact, he was so versatile that we converted him to a starting point guard his senior year and he led us to 27 wins while leading the conference in assists.

To some on the outside, I'm sure playing Curtis in the most pressure-packed moments of the season did not look right on paper during his junior year. But I trusted Curtis and the entire team trusted Curtis.

While he made big plays all throughout the season for us in this role, nothing was sweeter than our second round win in the NCAA Tournament over number two seeded Wisconsin in Chicago that sent us to the Sweet 16. Late in the game we found ourselves in a battle with the Badgers. Holding a small lead with 1:20 remaining, Curtis hit a 22-foot three-pointer as the shot clock expired. Our bench and fans erupted and momentum came back our way.

After Wisconsin cut the lead back to three, we took a timeout. This time, the play would be called for Curtis. We designed an isolation play for him against the smaller man who was guarding him. He took his man one-on-one and drained a 10-foot floater in the lane. The shot all but iced the win. We were going to the Sweet 16! **That day, Curtis Terry repaid us for our trust.** Trust he had earned.

Post-game

As a coach, you are forced to learn to put your trust in others because you cannot score points or play defense. You must rely on others to do that. As a leader in business or any organization, deciding whom you trust the most on your team may not be the first step.

The first step may actually be realizing you have to learn to trust other people rather than yourself.

Many leaders and entrepreneurs have the "I can do it myself" syndrome or its sister syndrome the "No one can do it the way I do it" syndrome. While it may be true that no one can do the particular job as well as you can, if you personally completing a project is not the most efficient way for you to be spending your time for the overall wellbeing of the organization, then that is not strong leadership.

Spend time finding out more about the people on your team. Try not to make assumptions. Instead, ask questions. Do they want more responsibility? Ask and you might be surprised when they reply, "yes."

Identify strengths and weaknesses of your team members. Be specific about the roles you want them to play. If you deploy people properly, they will perform well, thus, raising their level of confidence. This, in turn, will also help to expand their range of capabilities, which will enhance the performance of your team. Remember, success breeds success.

As a leader, your role is to make the people around you better. And to do that, you need to know what your team members are made of, what drives them. Stop wasting your time completing projects on your own and start investing your time into your team and coaching them on how to best accomplish the tasks at hand.

Throughout this process, you will begin to find out who the people you trust are. So when the game is on the line, you will begin to depend on them. And if you have done your job preparing them, **they will repay you.**

The Final Say

Pre-game

Many people can give input. Very few people, however, have the final say.

With the rewards of being the leader, who has the final say, come the responsibilities. Be prepared.

Game Time

The awakening was surreal.

There I was, 29-years-old and the new head coach of the men's basketball team at Texas–Pan American as well as the school's athletic director. It was my first head coaching position at any level.

This was a moment Barb and I had dreamed about and we were positive we were ready for the challenge.

Then it happened. Somebody with the school asked me to make a decision. And that is when it truly hit me — I was in charge. I had the final say.

As an assistant coach and even during my years as a veteran player in college, I enjoyed the freedom of having my opinion respected yet I was not being held ultimately responsible for the consequences of the decisions made about the team. There is comfort of being in that position. Ironically, we probably don't recognize the comfort when we are in that position. But once that comfort is gone and you become the person with the final say, you then realize the protection you had.

As the head coach, that level of protection was gone. Don't get me wrong, I embraced the new responsibility of being in charge. But as a first time top leader I did not properly anticipate the power of each and every decision that I made.

If I wanted to practice at a certain time that is what would happen. Think about that. For as long as I could remember I was a member of a team. I was told when to show up for practices and I would work my life around that schedule. This is how I lived my entire life. Now suddenly I was in control.

Recruiting. Traveling. Scheduling. Disciplining. Playing time. Where we were going to eat as a team. There were thousands of decisions to be made both big and small. And whatever I decided, that was the final word.

Being put in this position for the first time made me focus on the reality that there are consequences for every decision made. Many times, the most dangerous consequences are those that are unintended.

I was challenged to become much more methodical with my decision-making. I began to think more thoroughly and carefully through things. "If I make this decision, who does that impact positively or negatively?" The goal was to think two or three steps ahead to anticipate any potential issues.

What amazed me was that even with my experience as an assistant coach, I did not truly have a complete understanding of the impact of having the final say. As an assistant, I was much more focused on my areas of responsibilities. Many times I might push to try to improve something I was responsible for without understanding its greater impact on the entire program.

As the leader at the top, you do not have that luxury.

The lives of people are impacted by most decisions a head coach makes. That is not something to take lightly.

Post-game

Some people are attracted to leadership roles because of the opportunity to have the final say.

The best leaders, however, are in leadership roles because of the responsibilities that come with having the final say.

As a leader, the decisions you make for your team are final. You will ultimately be held accountable for the consequences of those decisions.

Surround yourself with good people and gain as much educated feedback and suggestions as possible. However, be methodical in your decision-making process and investigate all possibilities. As the leader, this is your duty.

Learn to anticipate the unintended consequences of possible decisions and actions. The best leaders are brilliant in this area.

A New Perspective

Pre-game

Strong leaders are not always in the top leadership positions. In fact, **the best organizations may have a number of solid leaders at different levels throughout the organizations**.

This can be a challenge for some individuals and organizations. Or, if handled correctly, it can be an amazing opportunity for everyone involved.

Game Time

After 20-plus seasons and 387 career wins as a head coach, I started the 2003–04 NBA season as one of Don Chaney's assistant coaches for the New York Knicks.

That was an ego check for me —not due to anything Don did. I was fortunate to be on his staff. However, being part of a staff and not being the main decision-maker on that staff was something I had to get used to again.

I had first served as a graduate assistant coach for Bob Johnson at Pittsburgh State at the age of 24 before heading back to my alma mater, Kansas State, to serve as a graduate assistant (1977–78) and as an assistant coach (1979–82). Then, at the age of 29, I was hired as head coach at Texas–Pan American.

Thus, from the time I was 29 until I was 51-years-old — a part of one's life when we make significant progress both professionally and personally — I became very comfortable with being the main decision-maker on our coaching staffs.

With the Knicks, however, that would not be the case. I would be lying if I said I did not wonder about how I would accept my new position of not having the final say. That is when I challenged myself by making a simple decision: "I wanted to be the assistant coach I would have liked to have working for me."

As I joined Don's staff, I decided everything

had to be about Don. This was an easy goal because Don is a very genuine person. He was easy to root for and most in our profession wanted to see him do well. Thus, I aimed to do everything I could to help Don be effective, successful and prepared.

My job was to make him look good in the eyes of other people. It all started with loyalty and, as the best assistant coach I could be, I was going to be 100 percent loyal to my boss, the head coach.

A management change midway through the 2003–04 season led to a dismissal of our entire coaching staff. However, I feel fortunate I had the opportunity to once again serve as an assistant coach after two decades as a head coach. It gave me a brand new perspective on unselfishly serving others.

Being an assistant coach does not come with a lot of the perks associated with being the head coach starting with the pay. However, assistant coaches are so important to the success of any program.

Without an amazing group of assistant coaches at every stop along our way, we would not have been able to enjoy the success that we have enjoyed.

As a head coach, I seek loyalty from our assistant coaches, and that is what they have delivered. Their job is to make me — the head coach — look good. To make me prepared, successful and effective. And they have done just that.

In return, it is my job to make them feel good about their contributions to our program and to help them receive the credit and notoriety they deserve. I take responsibility for helping them accomplish their goals professionally. For many of them, that means helping them to seek a head coaching position of their own. I currently have three former coaches heading Division I programs: Dana Altman at Creighton University, Kirk Speraw at the University of Central Florida and Tim Jankovich at Illinois State. They have all enjoyed success with their programs, and nothing makes me more proud.

Unselfishly, I must want this for them and help them seek these opportunities. Yes, this means we will lose great members from our staff, but the best assistant coaches and the most loyal assistant coaches need to trust that you are looking out for their best interests.

The beauty for all of us, however, is that everyone understands these opportunities for our assistants will become more readily available if our team wins.

We all have the same objective and that is to be successful together. And it all comes down to being loyal to one another . . . no matter your position.

Post-game

Solid leaders are not intimidated by other solid leaders. In fact, they seek them out to be part of their teams. This works because of loyalty.

A high-quality teammate (and leader) understands his job is to make other people on the team look good. In return, he must then trust the other people within the organization to help him look good. It is a complete team effort that is woven together by trust.

Unfortunately, not all bosses are strong leaders and not all strong leaders are bosses. This is something many of us struggle with within organizations.

Weak leaders in leadership positions often look to surround themselves with weaker people they can control. This allows them to protect their "leadership" positions. Unfortunately, this will ultimately lead to failure for the entire team.

A great leader is a loyal teammate whether you are in the final decision-making position or you are there to serve in a support role.

Take a look at your role from a new perspective. Who on your team can you help make look good? The best leaders live life confident enough to look through this lens.

Are you a confident leader? Do you want what is best for your employees? **Do your employees trust you to have their best**

interests in mind? The best partnership is a result of trust and loyalty that goes both ways.

Humility Is Healthy

Pre-game

Learning is not always easy and failure should never be easy.

However, much of the time the two go hand-in-hand. **That is if you are strong enough and humble enough to allow growth from your failure.**

Game Time

Being dismissed as the head coach of the NBA's Atlanta Hawks two months into our third season with the team was the most humbling experience of my life.

I had been fired for the first time in my career at the age of 50. Throughout all of our previous stops in the college ranks — Texas–Pan American, Kansas State, Florida and Illinois — we had enjoyed success in a short period of time.

However, the culture developed within a losing franchise in the NBA was a harsh reality to face. And, although there are many factors that go into the performance of NBA teams, I take full responsibility for not being able to change the culture within the Hawks organization in my less than two-and-half seasons there.

What hurt the most was we were so accustomed to being successful wherever we had gone. We had never failed to accomplish what we set out to do with a team . . . until Atlanta. It was both frustrating and disappointing to not turn the future with the Hawks. **So for the first time in my life I did not feel good about our efforts professionally.**

I remember going out to eat dinner in the days following being fired. Imagine one day your schedule being unexpectedly wiped clean for the next six months and having absolutely no commitments. Trust me, you have plenty of time to go out and eat. To this day I can vividly recall sitting at the table worrying that everyone in the room was thinking, "That's the guy who just got fired by the Hawks."

Despite all of the on-court and off-court successes we had enjoyed with four different college programs over the previous two decades as well as the comfort of knowing we had earned financial freedom for the rest of our lives, I was feeling as though I failed the Hawks. And on top of that, I felt that was what everyone else was thinking — starting with everyone else in the restaurant that evening.

If only I were that important!

The reality is there were probably just one or two people in the restaurant that evening who even knew who I was and, more importantly, didn't look at me as a failure with the Hawks.

Today, of course, I know this. However, when I was going through the challenge, I had no idea. Dealing with failure was brand new to me. And I believe I am a better man and coach today because of it.

Being humbled should be a healthy experience if you allow yourself to learn from it. What the Atlanta experience brought to me was a new perspective about what other people have had to deal with in their lives. As a coach, I had been fortunate to be successful with my first four head coaching positions. Meanwhile, when friends and associates were losing positions or battling tough situations, I didn't clearly understand what they were going through and how to best support them during their battles. Our unsuccessful run with the Hawks opened my eyes to a new side of our profession and what fellow coaches deal with.

It also revealed to me what most of us know — we perceive people to be much more judgmental of us than they actually are. I received call after call from people in basketball reminding me that this was the NBA, where basically every coach gets fired at one time or another. Although I was — and am still to this day — disappointed that we did not win with the Hawks as we had set out to do, the feedback from so many people helped me to better deal with any lack of confidence resulting from our failure.

Now when I see other coaches on the hot seat or see other coaches get dismissed, my empathy for them is at an even higher level. I understand the power of a phone call or a simple note of support.

Gaining a new perspective on life often comes from an initially humbling experience. But if you allow yourself to learn from the pain, you will grow as an individual.

Post-game

Secure leaders are humble leaders. They have made mistakes, have experienced failure and are now better people because of it. Moreover, they understand their team members will fail along the way.

As a leader, how you deal with failure is crucial. Not just your own personal failure, but the failure of your teammates as well. The key is to put you and your team in the best position to prevent failure from occurring again for the same reasons. One mistake should not lead to another mistake.

Lead with empathy. You have to constantly put yourself in the position of the person who failed and look at the entire situation from their viewpoint. Is there something you as a leader could have done better to help prevent them from failing? Effective leaders always address these issues first.

When dealing with failure, start with humility. It will be a more healthy and productive experience for everyone.

You cannot hide from failure — it will find you. Be prepared to deal with it and learn from it.

Moments of Crisis

Pre-game

It is inevitable that, as a leader, you and your team will periodically face moments of crisis. How you and your team react during and immediately following these moments will go a long way in determining your overall success.

While these moments of crisis are usually not planned for, a leader's job is to anticipate possible situations that may disrupt a team prior to this actually happening. Once a moment of crisis is upon the team, **the leader must proactively anticipate the possible fallout** and address each and every audience in a manner that is most productive for the overall and long-term wellbeing of the team.

Game Time

Following our 30-win effort with UNLV during the 2006–07 campaign, we entered the next season with many question marks about our roster. We lost five key seniors from the previous year's team, including centers Gaston Essengue and Joel Anthony, who combined to average 12.8 ppg, 7.4 rpg and 4.3 bpg.

Earlier in the spring of 2007, we were fortunate to have won a recruiting battle against the likes of Kentucky and Indiana for Beas Hamga, a highly rated seven-footer originally from Cameroon. It was a big signing for our program and it came on the heels of our Sweet 16 appearance.

Unfortunately for us, however, the NCAA questioned some of Beas' classes from his eighth grade year in Cameroon and ruled that Beas, who is a very smart young man, would have to redshirt his first year during the 2007–08 season.

That left our squad with very little depth in terms of height, having just one junior college transfer who measured in at 6-foot-10. After that, our bigger players consisted of a handful of 6-foot-8 and 6-foot-7 guys who were known more for their outside shooting than interior defense.

We knew going into the season interior defense would be a question mark . . . and that was before our moment of crisis.

Immediately following our team's first regular season game, our 6-foot-10 starting center was not pleased with his playing time and acted inappropriately in front of the entire team.

Unfortunately (especially because he is a very nice young man) his actions were so severe that keeping him on the roster would have been detrimental to the overall wellbeing of the team. The following day we made the decision to dismiss him from the squad.

He apologized profusely and sincerely. And, I must admit, if there ever were anyone we would have wanted to accept back on the team, it would have been him. He has a good heart, but the mistake made was not his first offense and it undermined what is at the core of our program. Keeping him on the roster was not a viable option.

Making such a decision, however, was not that simple.

To do so, we had to take into account all of those involved and try to anticipate the possible reactions and fallout.

First off, we had an obligation to protect the young man who we were dismissing. His life would be drastically impacted by this decision and our main concern had to be his mental wellbeing. At the same time we were serving as the disciplinarians, we also had to provide him the support he needed to move forward with his life. He ended up finishing the semester at UNLV before transferring to play for another school.

Secondly, we had to anticipate the reactions from the other players and understand these differed. Some might have been upset because you let a friend go. Others may have seen it as an opportunity for more playing time. And still others may have questioned if letting the tallest guy on the team go was the best idea for a team trying to advance to the NCAA Tournament in March.

Regardless of these individual beliefs, our message to all of the other players was that the excused player's actions were unacceptable and that **no one player is bigger than the team**. This is the message we preach throughout our program and, in our moment of crisis, we had to support that message. If any other players questioned the sincerity of our philosophy up until that point, we were sure it was answered with our actions.

Finally, we had to anticipate the reaction of the team's supporters. A lack of size was already a concern about the roster amongst the fan base and now we were letting our only true center go. While this was a concern, our core philosophy of being a disciplined, team-first squad had been resonating with the fan base for three seasons. And, after our Sweet 16 run just seven months earlier, we had earned the trust of the followers.

Overwhelmingly, the fan base and members of the media supported our decision to let the player go (without us getting into the specifics of the situation, in an effort to protect the player) while acknowledging it would make our season more challenging.

Would the fans and media have been as understanding had we not been to the Sweet 16 the previous season and not had a highly-touted seven-footer getting ready to play the next season? That we do not know. However, publicly, the perception of the program was protected by how we handled the situation.

Some may question why would public perception even be a factor in what some would simply consider a locker room situation? We disagree. Our program represents all of its stakeholders — players, families of players, the university, its students and alumni, the community, our fans — and we take great pride in trying to run a program that represents those audiences as best we can. Because of this, we run a very transparent program.

Because of this transparency, our actions in moments of crisis need to be consistent with our philosophy, made in a timely fashion and properly communicated to all stakeholders.

This philosophy was tested two more times during the 2007–08 season as we ended up parting ways with two other players throughout the year. All three of the players who ended up leaving the program were anticipated to have a big impact on our team coming into the season. But keeping them on the roster was not in the best interest of the long term success of the program and, possibly, not even in the best interest of the short term success.

Despite playing with a short bench because of the dismissals and being forced to start a 6-foot-7 player at center, Joe Darger (who was better known for his three-point shooting ability), our guys battled to win 27 games, repeated as Mountain West Conference Tournament champs and advanced to the second round of the NCAA Tournament.

Our coaching staff has taken a handful of teams further in the tournament and has won more games with other teams than our 2007–08 UNLV squad, but that team may have maximized its potential as much as any team we have ever coached. Our guys faced several moments of crisis throughout the year and responded together each time confident they could accomplish special things. When other people did not believe, our guys never doubted.

Post-game

Individual team members are just that — individuals. It is natural for each individual on a team to focus on his own wellbeing.

The job of a leader is to align each individual's focus with the overall focus of the team. The importance of this alignment is heightened during moments of crisis.

Any time one team member's individual wellbeing takes precedence over the wellbeing of the entire team — to a level that is detrimental to the overall success of the team — that team member should be removed from the environment.

This type of needed action is avoided many times by leaders in an effort to stay clear of a moment of crisis. Unfortunately, keeping this type of individual around can often lead to a constant state of crisis for the entire team, which is more detrimental than facing a moment of crisis.

Don't avoid moments of crisis for the sake of avoiding them. Confront them head on with confidence that you are doing what is best for the overall success of your team as well as with empathy for all of those involved.

Strong leaders don't necessarily like dealing with moments of crisis. However, they proactively address the situation in a timely manner while anticipating and protecting against possible fallout every step of the way.

One Final Lesson

Pre-game

There is a core philosophy we discuss that people always tend to be surprised when they hear. **We, as coaches, do not determine who plays or what roles our players will have. Instead, we simply evaluate the talent and performance of our players.** They show us — on and off the court — who will give our team a better chance of winning. Thus, the players themselves ultimately determine who gets the playing time and what roles they will play.

Game Time

Our players need to understand the power of this freedom. We do not control their futures, they do. The best players embrace this philosophy and take responsibility for their actions, both positive and negative. When things do not turn out the way they have planned, instead of looking for excuses, they seek action to improve upon the situation. Those are the types of players — and, more importantly, people — we want associated with our program.

As coaches, the only way to develop this environment is through trust. That trust starts by suppressing our egos enough to understand that we do not have the power to determine who plays or even the roles the players will have. It is out of our control. We lose the trust of our players the minute it is perceived that we are manipulating this process. If, in fact, one player earns the right to play over another player, those in the program cannot accurately question that decision. Our players are at all the practices, workouts, earlier morning lifting sessions and team meetings. They know who should be playing, who should not, who should be getting the shots and who should be handling the ball. Because they know this, it is crucial we get these decisions correct.

This philosophy is also true in the business

world. As leaders, we should not be giving out raises, promotions, preferred positions, nicer offices, better clients, etc. No, our team members should be earning these.

Not only is there a freedom in this for our team members, there is a freedom in this for us as leaders. We are not choosing our favorites — we are simply evaluating performance. The team members who give our entire team the best chance to succeed are the team members who should receive benefits — no questions asked. It is not based on outside factors, it is based solely on performance. This can be difficult for leaders at times because it may mean admitting we made the mistake by bringing the wrong person on board or putting someone in the wrong position.

When we fairly evaluate our team members based on performance, as leaders, our motives cannot be used against us. Sure disgruntled team members (i.e., team members who did not perform to the highest levels) may want to blame us for playing favorites or being unfair, but these complaints fall on deaf ears because the vast majority of the team will know the true circumstances.

This environment also raises the overall performance of our teams. Team members begin to worry less about competing against one another, which reduces the petty issues that drain organizations of energy, and begin competing to maximize their own individual potential.

263

Post-game

Many leaders inaccurately focus their attention and energies on getting the best results **for** their teams. Instead, we should be focusing on creating an environment that results in producing the maximum results **from** our teams.

Develop and maintain an environment that encourages your teammates to take ownership not only in their personal performance, but the performance of the entire team. Be confident enough to let them know — almost daily — that you are not in control of their futures. They are. Then prove to them it is true. Superior leaders are gifted at evaluating the talent around them and, more importantly, fairly and justly rewarding their team members based upon performance.

The sooner you give up this control the sooner you will find yourself in complete control of the direction of your team.

Sounds simple, right? **Now it's time to execute.**

Acknowledgments

Preparing these acknowledgements was one of the most difficult challenges of this book project. In an attempt at brevity, we will leave out people who have played tremendous roles in one of our lives. Please forgive us if you are included in this group and we ask for your understanding. We thank you for all you have done.

Lon Kruger would like to acknowledge:

Foremost, a special thank you to my parents, Don and Betty Kruger. They are both deceased, but they spent their lives ensuring that my brothers Mike, Dale, Jerry, David and sister, Terry, and myself had opportunities and foundations on which we could build our adult lives. Thank you.

John Punzo – our youth baseball coach in Topeka, Kansas. He helped to shape so many of us through his service.

Gene Wilson – a good family friend. Spent countless ballpark summer evenings discussing everything from baseball rules to world peace!

Paul Snavely – our elementary school principal. He has since passed, but many of his students have taken lessons from him throughout our lives.

From Silver Lake High School coaches Ellis Dahl and Joel Balzer as well as all of the classmates I ever had the pleasure to call teammates. Those high school days were special.

From my days as a player at Kansas State, Coach Jack Hartman, who has since passed. We shared a special bond and I will forever be grateful for the opportunities he gave me and what he taught me. A special thank you to all of the teammates (including classmates Danny Beard, Gene McVey and Larry

Williams) at Kansas State, both on the court and on the baseball diamond.

From Pittsburg State, Bob Johnson for giving me my first opportunity as a graduate assistant. Also, PSU president Tom Bryant and athletic director Bill Dickey.

From Texas-Pan American, president Miguel Nevarez and Judge Ricardo Hinojosa (who led the search committee) for believing in a young 29-year-old to not only lead their basketball team, but serve as athletic director. There is nothing more powerful than knowing that someone else believes in you.

From my time as head coach at Kansas State, Ernie Barrett. He is Mr. Kansas State – enough said.

From day one at the University of Florida, Bill Koss has been a good friend and advisor.

From Illinois, athletic director Ron Guenther. A good man and outstanding leader with an unyielding passion for the Illini.

Thank you to all of the men who have ever served on our staffs, especially Dana Altman, R.C. Buford, Greg Grensing, Gar Heard, Steve Henson, Lew Hill, Rich Hilliard, Tim Jankovich, Rob Judson, Rick Mahorn, Robert McCullum, Marvin Menzies, Eric Musselman, Mike Shepherd, Kirk Speraw, Randy Stange, Ron Stewart, Terry Stotts, Derek Thomas and Kevin Wall. You have made all of our days more enjoyable.

And, of course, a special thank you to all of the young men – and their parents or guardians – who have ever allowed us the honor to be their coaches. There are too many to even attempt to mention. Thank you for your hard work, your dedication and for making your basketball program a priority. Without you, none of this would be possible.

D.J. Allen would like to acknowledge:

My parents, Larry and Marilyn Allen, and brother, Nathan, for providing a foundation of team in my life. The Benson family for allowing me to be part of your loving team.

A group of friends that has made me a better player in life over the past two decades because of the team I have been on – Walt Denison (the ultimate teammate whose support of this project pushed it forward), Rod Dietrich, Dion Perez, Jim Seebock, Tom Stidham and Rob Tuttle.

The unselfish and talented team at Imagine Marketing – Alex Raffi (look at what you did), Amber Stidham, Ehsan Kaveh, Megan Lane, Jeff Jensen, Sue Burkholder, Wes Thurman, Melissa Rothermel, Nikki Williams and Gail Orta. Thank you for believing. You made this possible.

Jeff Johnson, Tyler Leavitt, Wolf Muchow and Nick Jones for helping to make dreams come true.

Brin Gibson for your wisdom and, more importantly, your friendship. Mike Tassi for teaching strength through compassion.

All of those who gave a young man a chance, including (but not limited to) – Pete Atkinson, Goldie Begley, Bill Bowman, Rodney Burr, Kirk Clausen, David Chavez, Ray Christensen, Bob Cooper, David Dahan, Stacey DeMarco, Tom Fay, David Gibson, Sr., David Gibson, Jr., Jim Gibson, Josh Griffin, Andy Hafen, Joe Hardy, Warren Hardy, Cindy Herman, Bob Kasner, Ray LeBoeuf, Don Logan, Fred Maryanski, Aaron Mayes, Scott Muelrath, Annette Mullins, Andrea Primo, Key Reid, Monica Simmons, Rick Smith, Spencer and Tessa Stewart, Paul Szydelko and Joan Tinker. Also, Alice Martz and the Henderson Chamber of Commerce; Rick Culley and Leadership Henderson;

Tim O'Callaghan, Colleen O'Callaghan-Miele and HBC Publications; and, Dr. Mark Wickstrom and Community Lutheran Church. To the rest of the Henderson and Las Vegas community, thank you for the support.

The Kruger family (Barb, Angie, Kevin and, now, Mike) and the Kruger basketball family – thank you for embracing the Allen family. It means more than you will ever know.

Both Lon Kruger and D.J. Allen would like to acknowledge:

Brian Rouff – without his guidance and support, this project would not be possible. You were our number 1 fan throughout the process. Thank you.

Carolyn Hayes Uber with Stephens Press — thank you for seeing the vision. Sue Campbell, Stacey Fott, Krissy Hawkins and Steve Guiremand for their work on this book.

To the entire UNLV athletic department, UNLV leadership and the Board of Regents. Thank you for your support.

All glory be to God.

Ordering Information

Quantity sales: Special discounts are available on quantity purchases by corporations, associations, and others. For details, contact the "Special Sales Department" at the Stephens Press address below.

Stephens Press, LLC
P.O. Box 1600 (89125-1600)
1111 West Bonanza Road
Las Vegas, Nevada 89106
(702) 387-5260
www.stephenspress.com

Individual Sales: Stephens Press publications are available through most bookstores. They can also be ordered directly from Stephens Press: (702) 383-0253; *www.stephenspress.com.*

Orders for college textbook/course adoption use: Please contact Stephens Press:
(702) 387-5260; *www.stephenspress.com.*

Orders by book retailers and wholesalers: Stephens Press books are available from major book wholesalers including, Ingram Publisher Services, Tel: (800) 509-4887, Fax: (800) 838-1149; E-mail: *customer.service@ingrampublisherservices.com;* or visit *www.ingrampublisherservices.com/ordering* for details about electronic ordering.

Colophon:

When it is available, we choose paper manufactured by environmentally responsible processes. These may include using trees grown in sustainable forests, incorporating recycled paper, minimizing chlorine in bleaching, or recycling the energy produced at the paper mill.

This book was typeset using Adobe Systems' ITC Glypha LT Std. typeface, designed by Adrian Frutiger in 1979. Glypha is a revival of the early English slab serif types, but more condensed and elegant.